JOURNEY TOWARDS EASTER

Cardinal Joseph Ratzinger

JOURNEY
TOWARDS EASTER

Retreat given in the Vatican
in the presence of Pope John Paul II

Crossroad • New York

Cover illustration
Michelangelo: The Risen Christ
Santa Maria sopra Minerva, Rome

1987

The Crossroad Publishing Company
370 Lexington Avenue, New York, N.Y. 10017

Originally published as *Il Cammino Pasquale*
Copyright © Editrice Ancora Milano 1985

Translated by Dame Mary Groves OSB

English translation copyright © St Paul Publications 1987

Printed in the United States of America

Library of Congress Cataloging-in-Publication Data

Ratzinger, Joseph.
    Journey towards Easter.

    Translation of: Il cammino pasquale.
    Includes bibliographical references.
    1. Retreats for clergy.   2. Lent—Meditations.
3. Jesus Christ—Meditations.   4. Paschal mystery—
Meditations.   5. Church—Meditations.   6. Priesthood
—Meditations.   I. Title.
BX1912.5.R3813   1987   269'.692   86-19811
ISBN 0-8245-0803-3

Contents

Preface

It is with pleasure that at the request of the publishers of this book I am offering to English-speaking readers the Retreat which I had the honour of giving before the Holy Father and the members of the Roman Curia at the beginning of Lent 1983.

In composing these meditations I was led by the thought that the forty days of Lent form as it were the great spiritual exercise which the Church presents from year to year, in pieparation for the great Paschal Mystery and to deepen our awareness of it. To make a retreat is to go into training to be Christian. In the same way that walking and running are a means of exercising the body, a retreat is a spiritual exercise which prepares the soul to make an ever better response to the call we have reecived. The central mystery of our vocation is the same as that to which Lent is leading: the death and Resurrection of the Lord. Thus the liturgical period in which this retreat was set was an invitation to us to look more closely at the sacramental dimension of our Christian life, and especially at the two properly paschal sacraments, Baptism and the Eucharist — the primary source and the normal food of that life. To enter into the mystery of Christ's death and Resurrection, celebrated and made present by these sacraments, demands however on the theological level an education in the faith by which each liturgical celebration is nourished, and at the same time, on the existential level, practical exercises in actually living that faith. That is why in preparing the retreat I endeavoured to assemble all the components of the liturgical texts (the readings are taken from the Cycle for Year C) which suggests the theme of a journey, of being on the way. Starting from this basic aspect I aimed at a study of the Paschal Mystery of Christ and his Church, which would nevertheless continue at the same time closely related to the actual circumstances in which the conferences were given. The reader will readily observe that the meditations (which for certain chapters take up and reformulate earlier works*) result from an underlying assumption — that in fact of the 'fides orandi' of the main Christian tradition — the conviction of an essential unity (as a distinction without a separation) to be found on the one hand between the Old and the New Testaments, and on the other between Christ and the Church. This is how for example I have shown the covenant rite between Yahweh and Abraham not only as an allegory of the radical commitment of the believer to the faith professed but, at a much greater depth, as the sign and precursor of another reality, inseparably historical and spiritual: the Cross by which alone is sealed the eternal covenant between God and the human race, reaching its effective fulfilment in the Eucharistic sacrifice. A similar Christological re-reading of the old covenant equates moreover to the view of the Church seen as being at once historical and spiritual. The people of God is truly the 'body of Christ' present in history; it is community in the Spirit, the 'new' people, which unceasingly acquires its reality from the inter-relation between the figure of the earthly Jesus and the mystery of the Risen Christ shining through it. Just as the two Testaments form the one Sacred Scripture, so are Christology and ecclesiology closely linked one with the other. Exegesis of the original sense of the Bible, however necessary it may be, does not receive its authentic Christian sense, save within the living Tradition attested by the Church's liturgy. On the other hand, the concept of the people of God taken up by the Second Vatican Council should not be understood as simply a sociological concept; it indicates, as the final

* The first two chapters of Part II, and the fourth paragraph of Chapter 4, equate in large measure to the second chapter of my little book *Der Gott Jesus Christi* (Munich 1976). For Chapters 3 and 4 of Part II and the first chapter of Part III I have drawn largely on my *Schauen auf den Durchbohrten* (Einsiedeln 1984) which has so far appeared only in German. Finally, the last chapter is based on a conference given at Cologne in 1983, on the occasion of the fiftieth anniversary in the priesthood of Card. Höffner. I have however tried to reformulate the various passages and to combine them in such a way as to give them an internal unity arising from the main underlying theme.

Report of the recent Extraordinary Synod has again reminded us: "the close communion of all the faithful in the (Eucharistic) body of Christ, which is the Church".

Such were the guidelines and basic premises of these meditations. It is my hope that this modest work may contribute to increasing joy in the faith and a more profound understanding of its teaching.

Rome, Feast of the Presentation 1986

Joseph Card. Ratzinger

Part I

Introduction to the Liturgy of the First Week of Lent

First Sunday of Lent

(Deut 26,4-10; Rom 10,8-13; Lk 4,1-13)

I

Jesus was led by the Holy Spirit into the desert (Lk 4,1): with his baptism Jesus entered on his public ministry as Servant of God, Lamb of God, Son of Man, Messiah.

To be baptised by John was an act of penance; an act which began with a personal confession of sins (Mk 1,5; Mt 3,6). Thus to go down into the river and be washed was a gesture of humility, a humble prayer for pardon and grace. In other words, that descending is a symbolic dying of the old life to obtain the grace of a new life. If Jesus, the Lamb without sin, joins the file of sinners lining up for the confessional, so to speak, if with that public gesture he makes himself one with sinners, receiving the sacrament of sinners, at that moment begins his hour, the hour of the Cross. Jesus becomes our representative and carries the yoke with us.

From then on there is no longer any private life for him; his life is fully obedient to the voice of the Spirit. His life is totally one of mission: representing our life before the Father; a life which is therefore intimately, to its spiritual depths, a life *for* us. In our baptism we have entered into his baptism. Christian baptism is the moment of our entrance into his death, in that 'for', which is the essence of the humanity of the Son of God. Consequently, to be baptised requires joining in the obedience of the Son, in the obedience of him who does, not his own will, but that of the Father, under the guidance of the Holy Spirit.

But let us go back to the text: the Spirit leads Jesus into the desert. What does this surprising guide intend? Let us reflect a little on what is meant by 'the desert'.

13

1. The desert is the place of silence, of solitude; it is the absence of the exchanges of daily life, its noise and its superficiality. The desert is the place of the absolute, the place of freedom, which sets us before the ultimate demands. Not by chance is the desert the place where monotheism began. In that sense it is a place of grace. In putting aside all preoccupations we encounter our Creator.

Great things have their beginnings in the desert, in silence, in poverty. It is not possible to share in the mission of Jesus, in the mission of the Gospel, without sharing in the desert experience, its poverty, its hunger. That beautiful hunger for justice of which the Lord speaks in the Sermon on the Mount cannot be born in the fulness of satiety. . . And let us not forget that for Jesus the desert did not end with those forty days. His final, extreme, desert was to be that of Psalm 21: "My God, my God, why hast thou forsaken me?" And from that desert sprang up the waters of the life of the world.

These conferences seek to be a desert interval in our work. Let us pray to the Lord that he will lead us, that he will make us find that deep silence in which his word abides (cf. Wis 18,14): "While gentle silence enveloped all things . . . thy all-powerful word leaped from heaven".

2. The desert is also the place of death: there is no water there, the basic element for life. And so this place, with its harsh burning light, appears to be the extreme opposite of life, a dangerous threatening waste. In the Old Testament, silence is an element of death: the human being as a person lives by love, lives by relationships, and precisely thus is in the image of the Trinitarian God, whose persons are *relationes subsistentes*, a pure act of the loving relationship of love. Next, the desert is not only the region which threatens biological life, it is also the place of temptation, the place where the power of the devil is manifested, the "murderer from the beginning" (Jn 8,44). Entering into the desert, Jesus exposes himself to this power, opposes himself to this power, continues the action of his baptism, the action of the Incarnation, descending not only into the depths of the waters of the Jordan, but descending moreover into the depths of human misery, — as far as the region of broken love, of destroyed relationships, in

14

that solitude to be found throughout the world marked by sin. A theologian of the fifth century said: Jesus descended into hell when he went before Caiaphas. . . How many times does Jesus not go before Caiaphas — still today![1] And so we may meditate on what it means to 'follow Jesus'.

On the other hand this descent of Jesus into solitude expresses the infinite love of God and confirms the marvellous words of Psalm 138: "If I ascend to heaven, you are there; if I go down into hell, you are there" (v. 8).

3. By entering into the desert, Jesus enters also into the history of the salvation of his people, the chosen people. This history begins with the going out from Egypt, with the forty years of wandering in the desert; at the heart of these forty years we find the forty days of Moses on the mount, the days of being face to face with God, days of absolute fast, days away from his people in the solitude of the cloud, on the top of the mountain; from these days flows the fountain of revelation. Again, we find the forty days in the life of Elijah who — persecuted by King Ahab — went forty days' journey into the desert, so returning to the starting-point of the Covenant, to God's voice speaking and a new beginning in the history of salvation.

Jesus enters into this history, into the temptations of his people, into the temptations of Moses, even as Moses offered the sacred exchange: to be blotted out of the book of life for the salvation of his people. So Jesus will be the Lamb of God, who carries the sins of the world, the true Moses, who is truly "in the bosom of the Father", face to face with him and revealing him. He is truly the fountain of living water in the desert of the world, he who not only speaks but *is* the word of life: way, truth and life. From on high on the Cross he gives us the new covenant. The true Moses, at the Resurrection he enters into the Promised Land, closed to Moses, and with the key of the Cross opens to us the gateway to that Promised Land.

So Jesus sums up the whole history of Israel. This history is *his* history: Moses and Elijah not only speak *to* him but *of* him. To be converted to the Lord is also to enter into the history of salvation, returning with Jesus to the beginnings on

Sinai, taking part in the journeys of Moses and of Elijah, which is the road to God and to Jesus, as Gregory of Nyssa has described it in his *Ascensus Moysis*.

Another element seems to me important, however. Jesus goes into the desert to be tempted, to share in the temptations of his people and of the world, to bear our misery, to conquer the foe and so to open the way for us to the Promised Land. It seems to me that all of this belongs in a particular manner to the sacred office: to be exposed in the front line to the temptations and necessities of any given time, to suffer the sufferings of faith at a given time with others and for others. If at a certain period philosophy, science, political power, create obstacles to the faith, it is to be expected that priests and religious should feel it even before lay folk; in the firmness and the suffering of their own faith and their own prayer they ought to construct the way of the Lord in the new desert of history. The journey of Moses and Elijah are always being repeated, and so human life is always starting out afresh along the road and the unique history of the Lord Jesus.

II

In this second meditation on the Gospel for the First Sunday of Lent, I should like to consider the central content of the text, which is the temptations of Jesus. What do these facts and mysterious words mean?

1. Let us make a preliminary observation which to my way of thinking offers the key to this inexhaustible story. In this extraordinary dispute, both the Lord and the devil use texts from the Old Testament. In a certain sense it can be said that the dispute over the true interpretation of the Old Testament is the essential content of this event. The central question of the dispute between Jesus and the devil is: who really owns the Old Testament? Does the Old Testament speak of Jesus or not? The Gospel says: the Old Testament read in company with Jesus is the word of God, the revelation of his salvific truth. The Old Testament taken separately from Jesus becomes

a tool of anti-Christ, the enemy, the disturber. In this context the fate of humankind is decided here, the dominion of the world and of history, as between God and the devil.

When St Luke or St Matthew were writing their Gospels, this dispute was not a thing of the past, but had rather all its actuality, on the one hand in the dispute concerning the Christian interpretation of Moses and the Prophets, and on the other in an interpretation which was concerned to demonstrate how none of the promises were fulfilled in Jesus, and that consequently Jesus was a usurper in respect of the Old Testament, an impostor, as the High Priest called him in Matthew (27,63). In a different fashion the same dispute remained the central problem of Christianity in the second and third centuries, when Marcion and gnosticism in general opposed the two Testaments: opposed the God of the Old Testament — who for them became the god of this world, that is, the devil — to the new God of Jesus; opposed the God of the New Testament — the God-revolution — to the world of the God of antiquity, to the Creator, called disdainfully the 'demiurge'. The problem returned in the last century, when Harnack, that protagonist of liberal theology, adopted the theory that in the time of Marcion to do away with the Old Testament was still premature, that even in the time of the Reformation recognition of the Old Testament as belonging to the Canon was inevitable, but that in our time it would be an inexcusable error to preserve this book of the Hebrews. In an inverse sense, the argument over the true significance of the Promise stands at the centre not only of present-day theology but of contemporary history. Today we have the atheistic interpretation of the Old Testament, in the philosophy of for example Ernst Bloch, which claims to be the true interpretation of Hebrew Messianism, in the light of Marxism and its atheistic and secularist messianism. The Liberation theologies of Marxist inspiration restrict Jesus to the Old Testament, invert the relationship of the Testaments and, instead of being interpreted as a precursor of Jesus, Moses the political liberator becomes the model of Jesus, who then appears as a sort of incomplete Moses. Not the Cross but the Exodus becomes central to Scripture, and the Promise, robbed of its spiritual content, returns to its earthly sense, the political.

17

This progressism is in fact regression, a return to Jesus' distant past, and thus it becomes also a cancellation of Moses and Elijah who walked towards the future — towards Jesus.

On thinking over this situation we see that the dispute in the desert between Jesus and the devil continues, that this story describes the reality of our times, shows us the roots of our present situation. And so it is that in the light of this text we can understand the signs of the times. In the scriptural debate is actualised the decisive struggle concerning human life, a struggle over humanity.

2. Let us consider now what the devil proposes, in what manner and in what sense it is that he interprets Scripture.

a) The devil proposes that Jesus should change the stones of the desert into bread, thus referring to the Mosaic miracle of the Manna. The Messiah, according to the rabbinical tradition, was to repeat it in a definitive form: the Messiah, that is, should give humankind everlasting bread, should do away with hunger, and create a world where all would have enough to eat, a world of complete prosperity. This would be the true sign of the Messiah, the true redemption of humankind suffering from hunger, the true and definitive repetition and re-enactment of the desert miracle. According to this interpretation, if someone satisfies all hunger and gives bread to all and for ever, this is the Messiah. The temptation returned after the multiplication of the loaves, linked now with the second temptation, that of power. The refusal of these two temptations signalised the beginning of the passion of Jesus. With this second refusal of the two temptations begins the *Via Crucis*, leading to the Paschal Mystery.

The devil's proposal is very plausible. Hunger is one of the most tragic of the plagues of humankind expelled from paradise. If we had to set about the redemption on our own, bread would certainly be for us the central problem in our saving of humankind.

And in fact: Jesus gives us bread; it is his central gift, but in a manner completely different from that proposed by Satan; Jesus, the grain of wheat dying for us, becomes bread. In the Eucharist the multiplication of the loaves will last until the end of time, when God revealed will be our everlasting bread. And so in Jesus who dies will be the sign of the Manna, and he shows himself to be the true, the definitive Moses.

But what is the real difference between the Eucharistic miracle, the divine miracle, and the miracle suggested by Satan? Iit is not easy to find the heart of this essential difference. Our Lord's reply, taken from Deuteronomy and its interpretation of the Manna, throws light on a central point: the primacy of the word of God for the salvation of humankind: "Man shall not live by bread alone, but by every word that proceeds from the mouth of God" (Mt 4,4; Lk 4,4). Without responding to the hunger for truth, without curing the malady of the soul wounded by deceit or, in a word, without truth and God, humankind cannot be saved. Here we discover the essence of the devil's lie: according to his view of the world, God appears superfluous, not necessary for the salvation of humankind. God is a luxury for the rich. The sole decisive thing is, according to him, bread: matter. According to him the person would centre on the belly.

The devil's lie is therefore dangerous, because it contains and renders absolute a part of the truth. Man does live *also* by bread, but not by bread *alone*. This reply of the Lord clarifies what the devil had suggested, that bread *alone* suffices. The hunger of the world is a terrible evil, but to remove *only* this evil does not reach to the root of the human malady. Jesus will in *his* good time multiply bread, but he multiplies it by means of love, which he distributes through his word, the word which opens people to the truth and so saves them in very truth. To put this differently: only God suffices; give someone all the good things in the world but withold God, and that person is not saved; that would not be salvation but deception and lies. And let us repeat once more, the devil's lie is dangerous because it has an incredible resemblance to the truth, renders absolute the more apparent aspect of the truth. Here we come to the point where our examination of conscience should begin, with a twofold aim.

That is, are not we also in danger of thinking that God is not necessary for humankind, and that technical and economic progress are more urgent than the spiritual? Have not we also thought that spiritual realities are less real than the material?

Is there not also a tendency to defer announcing the truth of God in order to do 'more necessary' things first? In fact, however, we see that economic development without spiritual development is destroying humankind and the world.

But how is it possible for us to think that God, the Trinitarian God, the Father, the Son incarnate, the Holy Spirit, and the concrete truth of revelation continued and lived in the Church, would be less important or less urgent than economic development? The impossibility of this thought shows itself if in reality our life is nourished day by day on the word of God. The devil's lie could enter into our soul if we in our personal life prefer material well-being to the grandeur and suffering of the truth. The devil could enter if God started to take second place in our personal lives. In the multiplicity of our daily tasks it can easily happen that God becomes secondary. God is patient and silent, those other things are urgent and demanding; it is much easier to put off listening to the word of God than to so many other things. Let us examine our conscience today and return to right order, to the pre-eminence of God.

Allow me, at this point of our meditation, to include an observation. Inseparably connected with fasting is the question of hunger and bread. Jesus' road begins with the forty days of fasting, as did those of Moses and Elijah. Jesus told the disciples that a certain kind of demon is not to be cast out in any other way than by prayer and fasting. Cardinal Willebrands told me that after the talks with the Monophysites, their patriarch in Egypt said at the end of his visit in Rome: "Yes, I have understood that our faith in Jesus Christ, true God and true man, is identical. But I have found that the church of Rome has abolished fasting, and without fasting there is no Church".

The primacy of God is not really achieved if it does not also include human corporality. The truly central actions of human biological life are eating and reproduction, sensuality. Therefore virginity and fasting have been from the beginning of the Christian tradition two indispensable expressions of the primacy of God, of faith in the reality of God. Without being given corporal expression also, the primacy of God with difficulty remains of decisive moment in a human life. It is true: fasting is not all that there is to Lent; but it is something indispensable for which there is no substitute. Freedom in the actual application of fasting is good and corresponds to the different situations in which we find ourselves. But a communal and public act of the Church seems to me to be no less necessary today than in past times, as a public testimony to the primacy of God and of spiritual values, as much as solidarity with all those who are starving. Without fasting we shall in no way cast out the demon of our time.

Let us return to our starting point, which was the intention of making an examination of conscience under two heads. The first was the question of whether God is really important and has priority in our actual life. The second point goes back to the multiplication of the loaves, needed in every age. Although the redemption we receive is not a purely material, economic and political one, we are conscious none the less of the grave obligation to arouse those spiritual forces which are able to change the world, to appease the hunger of so many of our brothers and sisters. We know that the earth has sufficient riches to satisfy all, we are not lacking in material goods: we lack the spiritual strength which could create a world of justice and peace. Why, again, are there so many poor among Christians, so many who hunger? Why does the *agape* of the Christians — the multiplication of loaves effectively mediated by love — not correspond to the Eucharist of the Lord? The Lord who shares in the hunger of even the smallest of his brothers and sisters will say to us one day: "I was hungry and you gave me food" or else: "I was hungry and you gave me no food" (Mt 25,42.35). Let us pray that we may recognise the Lord when he is hungry and has need of us.

b) With all these considerations, we have so far meditated on only the first of Jesus' temptations. For the purpose of this retreat it is not necessary to enter further into the interrelation of the other two, that of power and that of sensationalism. The pattern is the same: to bring about a redemption without God, without the truth, solely by means of earthly power and with the ingredients of material well-being. A paradise constructed in such a way is in truth a kingdom of the devil, a kingdom of lies. The crucified Lord, he alone, after

21

all, could say on another mountain: "All authority in heaven and on earth has been given to me" (Mt 28,18).

So, our meditation on the Gospel of the First Sunday of Lent coincides with St Ignatius' meditation on the Two Standards, today no less necessary than in the century of the Reformation. Let us enter into this meditation and pray that God will enlighten us.

Monday of the First Week of Lent

(Lev 19,1-2.11-18; Mt 25,31-46)

I

1. The prayer for today expresses in its opening words, in the shortest and clearest form, the programme for Lent: "God our Saviour, bring us back to you". This prayer corresponds to the first words of the Gospel of Jesus: "Repent. . ." (Mk 1,15), but changes the command form in Jesus' words into the prayer of weak human beings who know they cannot bring about their own conversion by themselves alone, by their own strength. By changing the command into a prayer, the Church also confesses this, and especially that this first step, conversion, is a grace: it is always God who acts first.[2]

"Restore us again, O God of our salvation", are words from Psalm 85,4 with reference to Jesus; in him the petitions of the Psalm have their answer: "Wilt thou be angry with us for ever?" In Jesus God has turned again and has given life; in him will his people rejoice.

'To be converted' means to follow Jesus, to walk with him, on his way. But let us again insist on the fact that *God* 'brings us back', converts us. Conversion is not human self-realisation, and we are not the architects of our own lives. Conversion consists essentially in that decision by which we cease to be our own creators, cease to seek solely ourselves and our self-realisation, but accept our dependence on the true Creator, on creative love: accept that this dependence is true freedom and that the freedom of autonomy emancipated from the Creator is not freedom but illusion, deception. Basically there are only the two possibilities for a fundamental option: self-realisation, in which we try to create ourselves, by possessing our being completely by ourselves, by having life in its totality exclusively for ourselves and through ourselves; and on the other hand the option of faith and love. This option is at the same time a decision for the truth. As we are creatures, we are not so by ourselves, we cannot make ourselves; we can only 'lose' our life or we can keep it. These options correspond to the content of the verbs 'to have' and 'to be'. Self-realisation wants *to have* life, all the possibilities, the joy, the beauty of life, because it considers life as a possession to be defended against others. Faith and love do not imply possession. They are options for the mutual interchange of love, for the majesty of truth. In brief, this alternative corresponds to the fundamental option between death and life: a way of life based on having is a dead life, full of dead things; only to cultivate love is to cultivate life: "Whoever would save his life will lose it; and whoever loses his life . . . will save it" (Mk 8,35).

We can also say that the alternative between self-realisation and love corresponds to the alternative in the temptations of Jesus: the alternative between earthly power and the Cross, between a redemption consisting solely in well-being and a redemption which is open to and relies on the infinite divine love. The choice of power expresses the attitude of moderns: they think that humankind ought not and can not expect help from God. For them it is time now to take history and the world into their own hands. Human beings themselves feel capable of constructing a free world, truly human. But meanwhile we are coming to see the consequences of this creativity emancipated from God and are thus beginning to rediscover the wisdom of the Cross. The Cross expresses the end of that autonomy which began in paradise with the serpent's words: "Become like God". The Cross expresses the primacy of truth and love, more important even than biological life. Even today the phrase holds good: *In hoc signo vinces* (By this sign thou wilt conquer); and starting from this choice we become good: God's goodness enters the world. And only the goodness and strength of God can build the Kingdom of God, which is also the true kingdom of humankind.

"God our Saviour, bring us back". The rejection of self-realisation and the primacy of grace expressed in this prayer do not imply quietism, but rather a new and deeper power of human action. Self-realisation is a travesty of life, considering it to be a possession, so that it becomes a service of death;

conversion is the action of choosing to make a response to love, openness to allowing ourselves to be formed by truth, to become co-operators with the truth as St John says (3 Jn 8). Consequently conversion is true realism, which makes us able for a work that is truly communal and human. It seems to me that there is plenty of material here for an examination of conscience. 'To be converted' is: not to seek after one's own success, not to seek after one's own prestige, one's position. 'To be converted' means: to stop constructing a personal image, not to work at constructing a monument to oneself, which would often end by becoming a false god. 'To be converted' means: accepting the suffering of truth. Conversion demands that truth, faith, love, become not in a general way but day by day, in the little things, more important than our physical life or than comfort, success, prestige and tranquillity in our lives. In fact success, prestige, tranquillity and ease are those false gods which largely impede truth and true progress in private and in public life. By accepting this priority of truth we follow the Lord, we take up our cross and share in cultivating love, which is to cultivate the Cross.

2. Let us consider briefly the other principal words in the prayer for today.

a) In this prayer we find the magic word 'progress': "Opus quadragesimale proficiat" (may the work of Lent, 'our observance of Lent", go forward). True progress is realised solely in following along Jesus' road, and taking the same direction with him. The heart of progress is progress in love. And love centres on the Cross, in losing oneself along with Jesus.

b) Moreover we find here the phrase 'work of Lent'. The original text of the prayer spoke simply of the Lenten fast. This is a wider meaning supplied by the new Missal, which seems to me apt. Fasting is not all that there is to the 'work of Lent'. It remains true however that discipline and ascesis are indispensable for human life, for true progress — discipline of the whole person, body and soul, as the prayer after Communion emphasises:

"Grant, O Lord, that this sacrament which we have received may bring strength and salvation to our bodies and souls, so that with joy we may experience in both the healing power of your grace".

This totality of Christian life belongs to the fulness of salvation.

II

Let us add further a short observation regarding the setting of the Mass for today. The ancient Roman liturgy had created a geography of the faith here, in this city of Rome, starting from the idea that, with the arrival of Peter and Paul and the finality of the destruction of the Temple and the rejection of the Lord on the part of the people, Jerusalem could be transferred to Rome. The consequence is that the geography also of the life and death of Jesus is written on the streets, on the spiritual physiognomy, of this city.[3]

3. Christian Rome is seen as a reconstruction of the Jerusalem of Jesus within the walls of Rome; more than a record of the past is contained in this fact. By impressing the features of Jerusalem on this city there is prepared here at Rome and in this world the new Jerusalem, the new city where God abides. And again we must add another thing here. This internal geography of the city is neither purely a record of the past, nor an empty turning towards the future; it describes an inner journey, the journey of ancient Rome to new Rome, of the old city to the new, the journey of conversion, which goes from the past through the crucified love of Jesus to the future. The new city has its beginnings in this inner journey, expressed in the network of Jesus' earthly journeys and of the history of salvation.

In this view is apparent the importance of the spiritual geography inherent in the 'stational' churches. The profound connection between the texts of the liturgy with these places forms a logical whole existential to the faith, which follows Jesus from the desert, through his public life, and finally to the Cross and the Resurrection.

The *statio* of today is at St Peter's ad Vincula. Three points are important for today's liturgy:

1. The church was built near a Roman tribunal. The idea of the tribunal, of justice, is thus present in this church: human beings are not left free in a void, as Sartre thinks, and as so many think today. Human beings are in the image of God, having their origin in a divine idea, and their freedom corresponds to this idea. God's central idea for men and women is love, and for this reason they will be judged according to the measure of their love. The tribunal expresses the eschatological aspect of the command 'Repent; be converted'; in it the message of the first reading and of the Gospel for today becomes as it were visible. This church is a visible sermon: earthly justice becomes open to eternal justice, to the last judgment.

2. On the other hand we know this church to have been constructed by the Empress Eudoxia to contain St Peter's chains rediscovered in Jerusalem; the church is as it were the noble storehouse of those chains and the custodian of a part of Jerusalem. The chains represent not only the passion of St Peter and the might of God, stronger than human power: they demonstrate besides the temptation of power, the limits of human justice; they speak to us of all the prisoners of the world, suffering in the cause of truth; they correspond to the words of the Gospel: "I was in prison and you came to visit me". The chains call forth the demand: "Did you come, do you come, to visit me in those who are imprisoned today for justice and faith? Have you been ready to bear human injustice for the sake of divine justice?" Today's stational church suggests prayer for the persecuted Church, for all those persecuted in the cause of justice.

3. The grandiose figure of Moses in this church emphasises these aspects for us, emphasises the harmony between the two Testaments, the harmony between Law and Gospel, between Moses and Jesus.

III

It is in this framework that the first reading (Lev 19,1-2.11-18) and the Gospel (Mt 25,31-46) should be interpreted. The two texts indicate the central theme of conversion, the point on which depend all the Law and the Prophets — the commandment of love of God and neighbour. By harmonising these two texts it can be seen that in fact the Law and the Prophets are nothing other than an exposition of what love implies.

In the New Testament we are set before this new fact, namely, that God himself carries out the commandment in the Son become man: God makes the 'stranger', this poor creature of a human being, his 'neighbour': becoming incarnate and dying, he assumes us into the unity of his person and in the history of humanity constructs the body of his Son — the Church. God in his Son comes to those in prison, becomes an outsider, shares in the world's hunger, and suffers death naked on the Cross.

So we come back to the prayer. To be converted is to follow Jesus, to be converted is to love, to be converted is to lay aside self-will and to open oneself to grace; the Law and grace are not opposed, but even say fundamentally the same thing. In this sense let us pray:

> "Put a new spirit within us, O God our Saviour. Form our minds by your heavenly teaching, so that we may draw profit from our observance of Lent".

Grant us to master not only the arts and sciences of this earthly life; teach us the true sciences: the disciplines of this same life, the disciplines of holiness, of heaven, of eternal life. In the mind of the Church, Lent is intended to be a compelling communication of heavenly teaching:

> "Form our minds by your heavenly teaching".

Amen.

Tuesday of the First Week of Lent

(Is 55,10-11; Mt 6,7-15)

In the liturgical texts for today is hidden the mystery of the Mother of God, intimately connected with that of the incarnation of the Son of God.[4] Let us look at the texts, and begin with the reading from the prophet Isaiah.

"So shall my word be that goes forth from my mouth: it shall not return to me empty" (55,11).

When the prophet Isaiah made this affirmation, it was not at all to bring out something merely trivial, but rather a contradiction of what might be expected. For this passage belongs certainly to the story of the passion of Israel, where we read that God's appeals to his people were continually defeated and that his word invariably remained fruitless, while God appears seated astride history, but not as a conqueror. For everything happened as a sign: the crossing of the Red Sea, the blossoming of the period of the Kings, the return of Israel to their country out of exile, all this now fades away. God's seed in the world seems to give no results. The prophecy, therefore, however wrapped in obscurity, is an encouragement to all those who in spite of everything continue to believe in the power of God, convinced that the world is not just rocky soil in which the seed cannot find room to grow, but certain that the soil will not always be only a thin layer on the surface, from which the birds day by day peck out suddenly what seed has there fallen upon it (cf. Mk 4,1-9).

For us Christians an affirmation of this kind has the ring of the promised coming of Jesus Christ, thanks to which the word of God has now truly penetrated into the earth and has become bread for us all: seed which bears fruit through the

29

ages, a fruitful response in which God's discourse has taken root in this world in vital fashion. It is difficult to find elsewhere the mystery of Christ allied to that of Mary in a form as clear and condensed as in the perspective of this promise: for when it affirms that the word, or better the seed, bears fruit, it means to say that it does not fall on the ground to rebound like a ball, but that instead it penetrates deeply into the soil to absorb the moisture there and transform it into itself. It thus takes the earth into itself, truly producing something new, transubstantiating that same earth into fruit. The grain does not remain alone: this is part of the fertility mystery of the earth — Mary, the holy soil of the Church, as the Fathers fittingly call her, belongs to Christ. The mystery of Mary signifies in this connection that the word does not remain alone; rather it assumes the other, the earth, into itself; in the earth of the Mother the word becomes man, and now, mingled with the soil of the whole of humanity, it can return again to God.

The Gospel on the other hand seems to be speaking of something quite different. Here it is a question of our mode of prayer, its correct form, its proper content, the way to comport ourselves, and genuine recollection: not so much therefore of what it is for God to do, but of how we ought to act before him. In reality the two readings are interdependent; we might say that in the Gospel we come now to see how it is possible for human beings to become a fertile field for the word of God. This they can become by preparing those elements by which a life can grow and mature. They attain this end by themselves living from those elements, thus transforming themselves, being impregnated with the word, in the word, immersing their life in prayer and therefore in God.

So this Gospel, then, accords with the introduction to the Marian mystery given by Luke, when in more than one place he says of Mary that she 'kept' the word in her heart (2,19; 2,51; cf. 1,29). Mary united in herself the various currents in Israel; in her prayer she bore within herself the suffering and the greatness of that history, to convert it into a fertile land for the living God. To pray undoubtedly means much more, as the Gospel tells us, than speaking without reflection, merely mouthing words. To be a field for the word means to be earth which allows itself to be absorbed by the seed, which assimilates

itself to the seed, renouncing itself so as to make the seed germinate. With her motherhood Mary transfused into it her very substance, body and soul, so that a new life might come forth. The saying about the sword which would pierce her soul (Lk 2,35) has a much greater and more profound meaning: Mary makes herself completely available as the soil, she allows herself to be used and consumed so as to be transformed into him, who has need of us in order to become the fruit of the earth.

In the Collect for today we are called upon to have a longing desire for God. The Fathers of the Church maintain that to pray is nothing else than to turn into a longing desire for the Lord. In Mary this petition is heard: she is, may I say, a vessel of desire in whom life becomes prayer, and prayer life. St John has wonderfully alluded to such a process of transformation while not calling Mary by name in his Gospel. He refers to her solely as the mother of Jesus.[5] She in a certain sense set aside whatever in her life was personal, so as to be uniquely at the disposal of the Son; and it is precisely in this that Mary realised her personality.

I think that such links between the mystery of Christ and that of Mary put before us by today's Readings are of great importance for the Western activistic mentality, which has reached its peak in our age. For to our way of thinking the principle of domination alone still has value: action, production, planning the world and, along with that, reconstructing it by ourselves, without owing anything to anybody but confidently relying on our own resources. With such a mentality, then, it is not by chance that we have more and more separated Christ from his mother, without taking account of how Mary, as his mother, could signify something indispensable for theology and for faith. The whole of this way of considering the Church thus starts out from an erroneous way of thinking. We may even ourselves consider it as a technical product which we intend to programme cleverly and bring to realisation with a tremendous expenditure of energy. We wonder whether that can happen which St Louis-Marie Grignon de Montfort appended to a passage from the prophet Haggai "You have done much but nothing has come of it" (1,6): "If doing takes the upper hand, becoming autonomous, then those things which are not manufactured, but are living and need to mature, will no longer be able to exist".

We want to get out of this one-sided outlook belonging to Western activism, in order not to degrade the Church to a product of our doing and planning. The Church is not a finished artefact but always living from God, needing to develop and achieve maturity. For this she requires the Marian mystery, just as she herself is the mystery of Mary. She can train herself to that fecundity only if she submits to that sign; only then does she become holy soil for the word. We should adopt the symbol of the fertile soil, we should become people who hope, harvesting their own inner lives, persons who, deep within their prayer, their longing and their faith, make room for growth.

Wednesday of the First Week of Lent

(Jonah 3,1-10; Lk 11,29-32)

At the centre of the liturgy for today stands the figure of the prophet Jonah; central also is the unity of the history of salvation, the unity between the Old and the New Testaments. Let us begin with the Gospel.

1. The Jews seek a sign from Jesus, a proof that he is truly the Messiah, he of whom Moses and the Prophets speak. They seek a sign and so repeat the temptation in the desert: Jesus is to give a practical demonstration, we might say, an experiential demonstration, that is, a demonstration drawn from material physical things. But to be redeemed, to place ourselves within the truth of the creative mind of God, we must rise above the region of physical, tangible things; not only rising above them but attaining to the new certitude of a reality more profound, more real — spiritual reality. This journey, consisting in abandonment and overcoming, is the one we call faith. The claim of physical proof, of the sign which excludes all doubt, hides a refusal of faith, the refusal to rise above the commonplace security of the everyday and thus also the refusal of love, because love of itself demands an act of faith, an act of self-abandonment.

The Jews sought a sign — we too are 'the Jews', just as much. Modern theology often stands looking for scientific certainty, in the sense of the natural, empirical sciences and, with this for a starting point, is obliged to reduce the Gospel message to the dimensions of such demonstrability. I think that an error such as this, on the level of demanding certitude, is what is at the heart of the modernist crisis, reappearing since the Council. Behind such a phenomenon stands a reduction of the concept of reality, and behind this tendency is to be found a spiritual reduction, a myopia of the heart too full of the search for physical power, possessions, having.

"This generation seeks a sign" — we too look for proofs, the sign of success, as much in general history as in our personal lives. In consequence we wonder whether Christianity has in reality transformed the world, has exhibited that sign of bread and security of which the devil spoke in the desert. The argument of Karl Marx that Christianity has had time enough to give demonstration of its principles, to give proof of its success, to give proof of having created the earthly paradise, and that after so long a time it is necessary to start again with other principles — this argument, I say, succeeds with many Christians, and many think it is at least necessary to begin again with a very different Christianity, a Christianity without the luxury of an interior life, of a spiritual life. But it is in precisely this way that we prevent the true transformation of the world, whose beginning is a new heart, a seeing heart, a heart open to truth and love — a heart freed and free.

The root from which this demand springs is egoism, an impure heart, which looks for nothing from God but personal success, help to make the 'I' absolute. This form of piety is a radical refusal of conversion. But how often we too depend on the sign of success, how often we demand the sign, and refuse conversion.

2. Jesus for his part does not reject every kind of sign, but he rejects the kind of sign demanded by 'this generation'. The Lord promises and gives his sign, the real evidence suited to this truth: "As Jonah became a sign to the men of Nineveh, so will the Son of Man be to this generation" (Lk 11,30). Matthew gives a slightly different emphasis from what appears in the Gospel of St Luke: "As Jonah was three days and three nights in the belly of the whale, so will the Son of Man be three days and three nights in the heart of the earth" (12,40). On comparing the two versions we find two aspects of the sign of Jonah renewed and fulfilled in the true Jonah: Jesus.

a) Jesus himself, the *person* of Jesus, in his words and in his whole personality, is the sign for all generations. This answer in St Luke seems to me a most profound answer, to be continually meditated afresh. "He who has seen me has seen the Father", the Lord affirms to Philip who asked: "Show us the Father" (Jn 14,8ff). We want to see, and so to be sure. Jesus replies: "Yes, you can see". In the Son the Father becomes visible. To see Jesus — this is the answer. We receive a sign, the reality giving proof of itself. And in fact, this presence of Jesus in all generations, the force of his personality attracting pagans too, non-Christians, atheists, is this not an extraordinary sign?

To see Jesus, learn to see him. . . This retreat is the occasion to begin afresh; and this is after all the sole and sufficient purpose of the retreat: to see Jesus. Let us contemplate him in his inexhaustible words, contemplate him in his mysteries, as St Ignatius provides in his Book of the Exercises: the nativity mysteries, the mystery of the hidden life, the mystery of the public life, the paschal mystery, the sacraments, the history of the Church. The Rosary and the Stations of the Cross are nothing else than a guide devised by the heart of the Church to learn to 'see Jesus' and thus to arrive at the answer of the Ninevites: repentance, conversion. The Rosary and the Stations of the Cross have been for centuries the great school for seeing Jesus; these days invite us to enter this school again, in common with the faithful of so many centuries.

Here also another consideration arises. The Ninevites believed the Hebrew's message and did penance. The conversion of the Ninevites is for me a most surprising fact. How are we to believe it? I can find no other answer than this: listening to the preaching of Jonah, we have to confess that at least the part of the message we can verify was plainly true: the wickedness of that city was great. And so we can comprehend that the other part also was true: wickedness destroys a city. Consequently we can understand that conversion was the only way to save the city. The evident truth required the sincerity of the hearers. A second element in the credibility of Jonah was the personal disinterestedness of the messenger: he came from a distance to perform a service which exposed him to derision, and certainly did not promise any personal gain. The rabbinical tradition adds a further element: Jonah remained marked by the three days and the three nights he had spent in the heart of the earth, in the 'belly of hell' (Jonah 2,2). The traces of his experience of death were visible, and authenticated his words.

35

Here some questions arise. Would we believe, would our city believe, if a new Jonah should come? God seeks messengers of penance even today for the big cities, the modern Ninevehs. Have we the courage, the depth of faith, the credibility, to touch hearts and open doors to conversion?

b) Let us return to the interpretation of the sign of Jonah in the synoptic tradition. While St Luke sees this sign simply in the person and the preaching of Jesus, Matthew underlines the Paschal Mystery: the Prophet who remains three days and three nights in the belly of the whale, that is in the depth of hell, in the abyss of death, prefigures the Messiah, dead, buried and risen again for us. The difference between the Evangelists is certainly not marked; the Paschal Mystery belongs to the person of Jesus so that aspect is not simply absent from St Luke. But St Matthew gives stronger emphasis to the mystery of Easter, to the creative force of God, revealed and demonstrated in the risen Lord, the real beginning of the new creature, the victory over death, the victory of love stronger than 'the last enemy' (1 Cor 15,26), death. God has in Christ worked an unheard of miracle: he has overcome death; Jonah returned from the 'belly of hell' — Jesus addresses to us the words: "Have faith, I have overcome the world" (Jn 16,33). God has finally heard the request of the rich man: "Then I beg you, father, to send him [i.e., Lazarus] to my father's house, for I have five brothers, so that he may warn them, lest they also come into this place of torment" (Lk 16,28). The true Lazarus has returned, we have no longer only Moses and the Prophets, we have Jesus, returned from the dead, to warn us; but Abraham's prediction remains true: 'If they do not hear Moses and the Prophets, neither will they be convinced if someone should rise from the dead" (Lk 16,31). Hardness of heart resists the sign of Jonah, too, the resurrection of Lazarus-Jesus. . .

The paschal element in the figure of Jonah is underlined also in the rabbinical tradition. There was a tradition according to which Jonah was to die in the sea for the salvation of Israel. He offered his death voluntarily: "Take me up and throw me into the sea" (Jonah 1,12); he did it, according to the Rabbis, because he feared that the pagans might do penance, be converted, obey the word of God, and so it could turn that God, comparing the penitence of the Gentiles with the obstinacy of Israel, would cast off his people. The death of Jonah — according to the Rabbis — was a voluntary death for the salvation of Israel, and therefore Jonah was 'just and perfect'.[6] The sign of true justice, of perfect justice, is to die voluntarily for the salvation of others. This sign Jesus gave. He is the truly just man. His sign is his death. His sign is his Cross. By it his sign will continue to the end of days, and this sign will be a judgment upon the world, a judgment on our lives. Let us, day by day and from now on, put our life under this sign; by making the sign of the cross at the beginning and end of our prayer, we receive and recognise the sign of Jonah.

c) One final observation. Jonah was annoyed by God's grace and goodness; he had announced judgment, and he was mocked. Is not this a danger for all pious people, a danger for us also, when we think that the practice of the faith is only for punishing others? Do we not perhaps ask: why the faith, if there is grace also for others? So we show that our faith does not spring from love of God, but expresses rather a love of self which seeks its own security. So we show that we have not yet undertood the sign of Jonah, the sign of the Cross, of dying for others. Let us pray God to make us understand more and more the sign of Jonah, love which triumphs over the world and over death.

Thursday of the First Week of Lent

(Esther 4,17; Mt 7,7-12)

In the liturgical texts for today the Church presents a catechesis on prayer. Queen Esther represents the people of God: in her anguish, exposed to violence from the powerful of the world with no power of her own, supported only by faith in God's might, she is led therefore to pray: "O my Lord, thou only art our King: help me, who am alone and have no helper but thee, for my danger is in my hand" (Esther 14,3-4).

In the Gospel Jesus invites us to prayer: "Ask, and it will be given you; seek, and you will find, knock, and it will be opened to you" (Mt 7,7). These words of Jesus are very precious, because they express the true relationship between God and humankind, and answer a fundamental problem throughout the history of religions and of our personal life. Is it right and fitting to beg something of God, or is perhaps praise, adoration, thanksgiving, a disinterested prayer, that is, the sole adequate response to the transcendence and greatness of God? Is it not perhaps a primitive concept of God and humankind, a more or less elevated egoism, if we ask good things for our life from the God of the universe? Jesus does not worry about this. Jesus does not teach an elect religion, completely disinterested. The concept of God taught by Jesus is different: his God is very human; this God is good and powerful. Jesus' religion is very human, very simple — it is the religion of the simple: "I thank thee, Father, Lord of heaven and earth, that thou hast hidden these things from the wise and understanding and revealed them to babes" (Mt 11,25).

The little ones, those who have need of God's help and tell him so, understand the truth much better than the intelligent who, refusing the prayer of petition, admit solely the disinterested praise of God, and in fact construct a human self-sufficiency, which does not correspond to the human necessity expressed in Esther's words: "Help me!" Behind this lofty stand which will not trouble God with our little needs is often found the doubt that God might not have the power to respond to the realities of our life, doubt whether God could change our situation and enter into the realities of our earthly life. In the context of our modern outlook on the world these problems of the 'wise and understanding' appear well founded. The course of nature is ordered by the natural laws created by God. God is not an arbitrary God; if these laws exist, how can we expect from God an answer to the daily necessities of life? But on the other hand, if God does not act, if God has not power over the concrete affairs of our life: how does God remain God? And if God is love, will not love find a way to answer the hopes of the loved one? If God is love and cannot help us in our actual lives, love will not be the ultimate power in the world, love will not be in harmony with truth. But if love is not the highest power, who is, or who has, the supreme power? And if love and truth are at variance, what ought we to do: follow love as against truth, or follow truth as against love? The commandments of God, whose heart is love, would no longer be true, and what contradictions would we not find then at the centre of reality? Certainly, these problems exist and accompany the history of human thought; the impression that might, love and truth do not go together and that reality is marked by a fundamental contradiction because it is inherently tragedy — this impression, I say, imposes itself on human experience. Mere human thought could not resolve the problem, and every purely natural philosophy and religion remain tragically inspired.

"Ask and you will be given". These apparently simple words of Jesus respond to the most profound questions of human thought with the assurance that only the Son of God can give. These words tell us:

1. God is power, the ultimate power; and this ultimate power, which holds the universe in control, is goodness. Power and goodness, in this world so often taken as separate, are identical in the ultimate root of being. If we ask: 'Where does being come from?'", we can reply with certainty: from

an immense power, or also — thinking of the mathematical structure of being — from a powerful and creative reason. Following the words of Jesus we can add: this ultimate power, this supreme reason, is at the same time pure goodness and the source of all our confidence. Without this faith in God the Creator of heaven and earth, Christology would remain fragmented; a redeemer without power, a redeemer divorced from the Creator would not be in a position to give us true redemption. And therefore we glorify the immense glory of God. Prayer and praise are inseparable, prayer is the concrete recognition of God's immense power and glory.

As I have already emphasised, we also find here the basis of Christian morality. The commandments of God are not arbitrary; they are, simply, the concrete exposition of the demands of love. But love also is not an arbitrary choice; love is the substance of being: love and truth. "One who knows the truth, knows that Light, and one who knows that Light, knows Eternity. Love knows it. O eternal truth and true love and beloved eternity", says St Augustine, when he is describing the moment he discovered the God of Jesus Christ (*Confessions* VII 10,16). Being itself does not speak only the language of mathematics; being itself has a moral content, and the commandments translate the language of being and of nature into human language.

This consideration seems to me fundamental in view of the present situation, in which the physical-mathematical world and the moral world look to be almost entirely separated. Nature seems empty of a moral language, ethics is declining into a utilitarian calculation, and an empty freedom is destroying humanity and the world.

"Ask and it will be given you", that is, God is power and love, God can give and does give. These words invite us to meditate on the ultimate identity of power and love; they invite us to love the power of God: "We give you thanks, we praise you for your glory".

2. God can hear and speak: that is, God is a person. This statement is at the heart of a clear Christian tradition, but an important current in the history of religions is opposed to such a concept and is becoming more and more a temptation for the

Western world: the religions arising from the Hindu and Buddhist traditions, and the gnostic phenomenon with its separation of creation and redemption. Today we are seeing a revival of gnosticism, which is perhaps the most sombre threat to the spiritual and pastoral work of the Church. Gnosticism allows of retaining the time-honoured terminology and ceremonial of religion, the aura of religion, without retaining faith. And this is the profound temptation of gnosticism: it is nostalgia for the beauty of religion but it is also weariness of the heart, which no longer has the strength of faith. Gnosis presents itself as a refuge where religion can continue after faith has been lost. But behind that flight stands almost always a faint-heartedness which no longer believes in the power of God over nature, in the Creator of heaven and earth. And so there begins a contempt of bodily things — the body appears exempt from morality. Contempt for the body generates contempt for the history of salvation, to become finally a religious impersonalism. Prayer is replaced by interior exercises, the search for the void as a place of freedom.

"Ask and it will be given you" — the 'Our Father' is the concrete application of these words of Our Lord. The 'Our Father' embraces all the true desires of humankind, from the Kingdom of God down to daily bread. This fundamental prayer is thus the indicator which shows the road to human life. In prayer we do the truth.

3. One final aspect opens to us, if we compare the text of St Matthew with that of St Luke and with the kindred texts of St John. St Matthew concludes his catechesis on prayer with the words of Jesus: "If you then, who are evil, know how to give good gifts to your children, how much more will your Father who is in heaven give good things to those who ask him!" (7,11). We find underlined here the absolute goodness of God, we find expressed the personality of God, a Father to his children; we find also an allusion to original sin, to the corruption of bad people, because of their rebellion against God, on the road to autonomism to the 'becoming like God'.

But for the moment our interest is not directed towards these fundamental elements of Christian theology and anthropology. Instead what concerns us is the following problem:

What are the possible subjects for Christian prayer? What things can we ask from God's goodness? The Lord's reply is very simple: everything. Everything that is good. The good God gives only good things, but his goodness in this knows no limits. This answer is very important. With God we can really speak as children to their Father. Nothing is excluded. The goodness and power of God knows only one limitation: evil. But it knows no boundary between big and little things, between material and spiritual things. God is human — God is man, and could become man, because his love and his power embrace for eternity the big and the little things, the body and the soul, daily bread and the Kingdom of Heaven. Christian prayer is completely human, prayer in communion with the God-man, with the Son. The prayer of the simple is the true Christian prayer, that prayer which with a fearless confidence brings all the reality and the poverty of life under the eyes of omnipotent goodness. We can ask all that is good. But as part of this unboundedness, prayer is a road to conversion, the way of divine education, the way of grace: by praying we must learn which things are good or not; we have to learn the absolute difference between good and evil, we have to learn to renounce all evil, fulfil our baptismal promises: "I renounce Satan and all his works". Prayer separates light from darkness in our life and accomplishes in us the new creation, makes us new beings. Therefore it is so important that in prayer we do in fact present our whole life before the eyes of God, we who are evil, who desire so many bad things. In prayer we learn renunciation of our own desires, we begin to desire good things, to become good by talking to him who is goodness itself. The divine response is not simply a confirmation of our life but a process of transformation.

If we discern the profundity of this very simple reply of the Lord in the Gospel of St Matthew, we can understand the special shade of meaning in the Lucan tradition. The Lord's reply according to St Luke runs thus: "If you then who are evil know how to give good gifts . . . how much more will the heavenly Father give the Holy Spirit to those who ask him" (11,13). Here the content of Christian prayer is much more limited, defined in a more precise manner than in St Matthew: the Christian asks from God's goodness not any kind of thing, but asks of God the divine gift — the Holy Spirit; asks of God no less than God himself — goodness itself, love itself — the God who gives himself — the Holy Spirit. Fundamentally this is not contrary to the tradition of St Matthew. According to St Luke also, good has to be asked from God: the good which embraces all good things. But St Luke shows himself concerned that human things should remain within the sphere of human responsibility itself; that prayer should not become a pretext for human laziness; that we should not ask too *little* from God, but that we should ask all — God himself — with the boldness of his Son. Thus St Luke underlines more than does St Matthew the purification of the desires proper to Christian prayer; he emphasises that the prayer *of God's children* is the prayer *of his Son*, a Christological prayer 'through Christ'. St Luke does not limit God's power to spiritual and supernatural things: the Holy Spirit penetrates *all*; but the actual object of prayer is emphasised: that we evil people should cease to be evil and become good by sharing in God's goodness itself. This will be the true answer to prayer, if we not only *have* the good things, but *are* also good ourselves.

We find the Johannine tradition to be along the same lines. St John draws out two aspects:

a) Christian prayer is prayer in the name of the Son. If the identity of the prayer of the children of God and of the Son of God in St Luke is only indicated, in St John this essential element becomes explicit. To pray in the name of the Son is not a mere formula, not mere words; to have part in this name requires following a path of identification, the way of conversion and of purification, the road to becoming Son; the actualisation, that is, of our baptism into lasting penitence. We thus reply to the Lord's invitation: "I, when I am lifted up from the earth, will draw all men to myself" (Jn 12,32). When we pronounce the liturgical formula 'Through Christ our Lord', all this theology is present; day by day these words invite us to the way of identification with Jesus the Son, to the baptismal journey, that is, to conversion and penitence.

b) St John indicates the content of prayer, its content of promise and fulfilment, by the word 'joy': "Ask, and you will receive, that your joy may be full" (16,24). And so this text can serve as intermediary between the tradition of St Matthew and that of St Luke. The aim of all our requests, all our desires, is joy, happiness; all the individual requests look for scraps of happiness. And so St John says to us with St Matthew: ask all from God — always look for happiness and the Father has the power and the goodness to give it. With St Luke, John says: all good things are fragments of this unique reality which is joy; and joy is finally nothing other than God himself, the Holy Spirit. Aim at God, seek 'joy', the Holy Spirit, and have all.

Thus meditation on the Gospel leads us to the opening prayer of the Mass of today: "Pour out your grace upon us, Lord, so that we may always recognise what is right and be prompt to carry it out. Thus may we learn to live according to your will, since we cannot exist without you".

Friday of the First Week of Lent

(Ezek 18,21-28; Mt 5,20-26)

The Liturgy of the Word for today is a catechesis on Christian justice, a response to the question: What is just in the eyes of God? How can we be justified? Thus we find also the reply to the question of the Law, the definition of the new law, the law of Christ, and the relationship between the law and the spirit; all of this is contained in the unity of salvation, which knows a progression, a purification, a deepening, but not an opposed dialectic.

I

The catechesis begins with the reading from the prophet Ezekiel, who provides a great step forward in the development of the biblical concept of justice. Two themes seem to me important.

1. The God of the Old Testament too is a God of love, a true Father to his creatures. This God *is* life, and death is therefore the total contradiction of the reality of God. God will not have his opposite. Consequently God is God of life for his creatures also. The death of the creature is — in human terms — a frustration for God, it is a withdrawal from him. And so God seeks for his creature, not punishment, but life in its full sense: communication, love, fulness of being, sharing in the joy of living, in the grace of being. "Have I any pleasure in the death of the wicked, says the Lord God, and not rather that he should turn from his way and *live*?" (Ezek 18,23). Here we are listening to that same God who speaks with the voice of the prophet Hosea: "How can I give you up, O Ephraim! How can I hand you over, O Israel! . . . My heart recoils

within me, my compassion grows warm and tender. I will not execute my fierce anger, . . . for I am God and not man, the Holy One in your midst, and I will not come to destroy" (Hos 11,8-9).

In this marvellous text we meet two key words of biblical soteriology:

a) The compassion of God: St Bernard of Clairvaux has found the formula fully corresponding to the biblical testimony: "Impassibilis est Deus, sed non incompassibilis"[7] (God cannot suffer but can suffer with those who do). The holy Doctor has, like the Fathers of the Church, resolved the problem of God's *apatheia*: there is *one* passion in God: love; and love in relation to fallen humanity is compassion and pity. We find here the theological foundations of the passion, of the whole of soteriology.

b) The heart of God: "My heart recoils within me" (Hos 11,8). On the one hand God has to set things straight, he must, in accordance with his own truth, punish sin; but on the other hand "my heart recoils within me" — the God of life, the spouse of Israel, could not destroy life, could not give free vent to his burning anger, and so he stands at odds with himself. The mystery of the open heart of the Son, the mystery of the God who in his Son takes upon himself the curse of the Law so as to free and to justify his creature, is already outlined in this text. It is no exaggeration to say that these words from the heart of God are a first and important foundation to the devotion to the Sacred Heart.

From Ezekiel and Hosea there is a direct line to the Gospel of St John: "For God so loved the world that he gave his only Son, that whoever believes in him should not perish but have eternal life" (3,16) — and to the accomplishment of these words in John: "One of the soldiers pierced his side with a spear, and at once there came out blood and water" (19,34).

If at this stage of our reflection we look for a reply to what is the measure of justice according to these texts, we can say: If God is essentially life, we correspond to him by our undertaking for life, our struggle against the dominion of death, in all its guises, and by our undertaking of life in its fulness, and of the reign of truth and love.

46

2. The second important point which the text from Ezekiel brings out is the clear and decisive personalism. This text signifies completely overcoming any kind of primitive collectivism, by which individuals inevitably form part of their clan, their social group, and can have no personal destiny distinct from that of the clan. Here we can see the emancipation, the liberation, of the person, with the person's unique and singular destiny. This liberation, the discovery of the uniqueness of the person, is at the heart of any freedom. This liberation is the fruit of faith in a God who is a Person, or better: this liberation results from the revelation of the Personal God. Liberation, and with that freedom itself, vanishes — not suddenly, but with an inevitable logic — at the point where this God disappears from the world's eyes. This God is not — as say the Marxists — a means to slavery; history shows us the contrary: on the presence of the personal God depends the indestructible value of the human person.

God loves us as persons, God calls us with a personal name, known only to him and to the person called. It is unfortunate that verse 20 of chapter 18 in Ezekiel is missing from the new Lectionary, for it expresses the essence of this new prophetic personalism: "The one who has sinned and not another shall die". This text has a special significance on the second Friday of Lent. Friday is always a reminder of the Friday of Jesus' death, and the Fridays of Lent underline this remembrance, directing souls week by week more and more towards the moment of Redemption. "The one who has sinned and not another shall die" — with this sentence God refutes the vendetta principle and substitutes a strictly personal justice (and also, the phrase "an eye for an eye, a tooth for a tooth" [Mt 5,38] has its part in this history of overcoming collective vendettas).

"The one who has sinned shall die and not another" — on Good Friday the Sacred Heart of God will break, and the only one without sin, the incarnate Son, will die for us. This voluntary death of one who is innocent in place of us sinners is not a refusal of the prophetic personalism but it gives it greater depth of meaning; the death is the 'abundance' of the new justice about which the Gospel speaks today. "The one who has sinned and not another shall die" — today, a Friday in Lent, let us gaze upon "him whom they have pierced", the one who died sinless and for us. Mirrored in his wounds we see our sins and we see his name, the abundance of the divine justice. The dying Son does not do away with justice, he dies to preserve it — his justice is as it were so abundant that it is sufficient for us sinners also.

II

Let us take another glance at the Gospel for today. Its key word, the key to the whole Sermon on the Mount, is the word we have already emphasised: 'abundance'. "Unless your justice exceeds that of the scribes and Pharisees, you will never enter the kingdom of heaven" (Mt 5,20). The new justice of the New Testament is not simply an advance on pre-Christian justice, it is not merely the addition of new obligations to those already existing; this new justice has a new structure, a Christological structure, the structure of abundance, the heart of which is already revealed by the word 'for': "my body offered in sacrifice *for* you", "my blood shed *for* you".

In order to clarify the meaning of the word let us meditate briefly on two important signs wrought by Jesus. In the episode of the miracle of the multiplication of the loaves there is mention of a 'surplus' of seven baskets full (Mk 8,8). Apposite to the central intention of the accounts of the multiplication of the loaves is the focussing of the attention on the idea and reality of superabundance, of that which is more than the necessary. This brings at once to mind the recollection of a kindred miracle, reported for us in the Johannine tradition: the turning of water into wine at the wedding in Cana (Jn 2,1-11). The term 'abundance' does not appear, but the substance of it is all the more realistically brought out: according to the data given in the Gospel the miraculous wine would measure in the region of 480–700 litres, which must surely be exorbitant for a private occasion! Both accounts make a further reference, according to the mind of the

Evangelist, to that central form of Christian worship, the Eucharist, and present it as the typically divine superabundance — the superabundance which is the expression, the language, of God's love. God does not give a something or other: God gives himself. God is abundance because he is love. God in Jesus Christ is the 'for us', and so demonstrates his true divinity. The abundance — the Cross — is the sign of the Son.

Thus we see that the measure of justice according to the Sermon on the Mount is the Christological measure — the Son. Even if the Sermon on the Mount does not explicitly speak of the Son, it is by its structure a profound Christological instruction, incomprehensible without the key of *Christology*. An abounding justice does not mean adding casuistry and laws. Justice abounding is justice according to the model of the Lord, justice by following Jesus. Or, in other words: abounding justice is a justice stamped intimately with the principle 'for'. As Christians we know ourselves to be sinners in need of the divine pardon. We know that we live by the love of "the Son of God, who loved me and gave himself for me" (Gal 2,20); not seeking self-realisation and to be the architects of our lives, or as people not in need of the love and pardon of others. On the contrary, Christians accept the need, accept the grace and, by accepting it, become free of self, able to give themselves, to give above what is necessary, in conformity with the divine generosity. So the Christian has the joy of abundance, the freedom of the redeemed.

Everything else contained in the Gospel for today is no more than an exemplification of the principle of abundance: the Christian interpretation of the Decalogue, which does not abolish but complements the Law and the Prophets (Mt 5,17).[8]

One further observation in regard to the Christological structure of the Sermon on the Mount. Significant for the new law in Jesus given on this new Sinai of his preaching is the antithesis: "... it was said to the men of old — but I say to you". With these words Jesus reveals himself as the new Moses. With him begins the new convenant, complementing the promises given to the Patriarchs: "The Lord your God will raise up for you a prophet like me from among you, from your brethren — him you shall heed" (Deut 18,15). The other saying at the end of Deuteronomy, which sounds like the lament of suffering Israel, like an urgent prayer that God should remember his promises: "There has not arisen a prophet since in Israel like Moses — whom the Lord knew face to face" (Deut 34,10), this saying full of sadness and resignation is excelled by Gospel joy. The new Prophet has arisen, he whose sign it is to be face to face with God. The contrast with Moses implies this sublime reality, implies that the essential characteristic of the new Prophet is speaking to God face to face, as a friend.

But Christ according to this Gospel is more than a Prophet, more than a Moses. To 'see' this message in the Gospel we have to read it with most close attention. The antithesis is not: 'Moses said', 'I say'; the antithesis is: '*was* said', 'I say'. This passive voice 'was said' is the Hebrew form veiling the name of God. In order to avoid the holy name and also the word 'God' the passive was used, and everyone knew the subject not named is God. In our language the antithesis has to be translated: "*God* said to the men of old — but *I* say to you". This affirmation corresponds exactly to the historical and theological reality, because the Decalogue was not given by Moses but by God, of whom Moses was only the mediator. Thinking over this discovery we find something remarkable: the antithesis is 'God said', 'I say'; Jesus is thus speaking on a level with God, not as a new Moses only, but with the authority of God himself. This 'I' is a divine I. Even Protestant exegetes admit that no other interpretation is possible, and that these words cannot be an invention of the primitive Church, which had rather the tendency to lessen contrasting statements. God spoke to the people of old; to us the same God, in the I of Christ, does not say something different, yet it is a new thing: "The old has passed away, behold, the new has come" (2 Cor 5,17). The Lord of the Sermon on the Mount is the same as he of whom St Paul speaks in these words, the same of whom the Revelation of St John speaks: ' Behold, I make all things new" (Rev 21,5).

Harmonising with these testimonies we have likewise the prayer after Communion for today: "You have given us, Lord, your holy sacrament to be our food. Grant that it may renew our strength and purify us from our old faults, so that we may be united with Christ, who is the source of our salvation".

Saturday of the First Week of Lent

(Deut 26,16-19; Mt 5,43-48)

With the Collect for this Saturday we return to the beginning of this week. Central to this prayer are the words: 'Turn our hearts to you'. So the connecting thread, the purpose of Lent, appears again: conversion. All the Lenten texts are interpretations and applications of this reality on which our whole life depends.

1. As in the prayer for Monday, so in this text, conversion is a gift, a grace: we ask God for the gift of conversion. A new shade of meaning is to be found in the address 'Eternal Father'. The prayer indicates the direction of conversion: we want to return to our Father's house; conversion is a returning. In conversion we seek the Father, the house of our Father, our native land. With these words ("turn our hearts to you") the prayer alludes to the classic description of the road to conversion, the parable of the Prodigal Son. This man does not simply leave, not only his body is in a far country — his *heart* is there, too. In his arrogance, in his loss of his true self, he has become a stranger, has left his home. In his life of forgetfulness of God and of himself, he lives far from his Father, in the 'regio dissimilitudinis' as the Church Fathers say, in the shadow of death. Life away from truth is the road to death; consequently the return to the fatherland also begins with an inner pilgrimage: the Son finds the truth again. "This seeing in the truth is true humility", says the Encyclical *Dives in misericordia*.[9] Such an interior journey is finally realised in the confession: "Father, I have sinned against heaven and before you". Confession is 'doing the truth', says St Augustine, interpreting St John: "He who does what is true comes to the light" (Jn 3,21). The recognition of truth takes place in con-

fession; in confession we come to the light; in that confession which took shape in a far country, the son covers the distance, scales the abyss, separating him from his home; in that confession he comes back to the truth and so to the love of the Father, who loves the truth, who is truth; love of the Father is what opens the door to the truth.

When meditating on this parable, we should not forget the figure of the elder son. In a certain sense he is not less important than the younger son, so that it is possible and even perhaps rather better to speak of the *parable of the two brothers*.[10] With the figure of the two brothers the text takes its place in a long biblical history which begins with the story of Cain and Abel, is taken up again with the brothers Isaac and Ishmael, Jacob and Esau, and is reinterpreted in various parables of Jesus. In the preaching of Jesus the figures of the two brothers reflect above all the problem of Israel and the pagan world. It is also not difficult to discover in the parable the pagan world in the figure of the younger son, his life spent far from God. The Letter to the Ephesians for example says to the pagans: "You, who were far off" (Eph 2,17). The description of the sins of the pagan world, given in the first chapter of the Letter to the Romans, sounds like a list of the vices of the prodigal son. Equally, it is not difficult to see in the elder son the chosen people, Israel, always remaining faithful in their Father' house. The elder son is Israel expressing his bitterness at the moment of the calling of the pagans, without having to fulfil the obligations of the Law: "Lo, these many years I have served you, and I never disobeyed your commands" (Lk 15,29). He is Israel, indignant and not wanting to take part in the wedding feast of the Son in the Church. In the words of this parable: "Son, you are always with me, and all that is mine is yours" (v. 31), God's mercy invites Israel, calls to Israel to come in.

But the significance of this elder brother is wider still. He represents in a certain sense the devout person, those, that is, who have remained with the Father and have not transgressed his commands. At the moment of the sinner's return he allows envy to arise, to become in the end a secret poison in the depths of his heart. And why this envy? Envy shows that many 'pious folk' cherish in the same way deep in their hearts the

53

desire for 'foreign parts' and what they promise. Envy shows that such persons have not really understood the beauty of their own home, the happiness of 'all that is mine is yours', the freedom of the one who is son and heir; and so it appears that they nevertheless secretly desire the happiness of a far country, that they have in desire gone off to that country; and they do not know it, will not recognise it. Consequently their loss of truth is still more dangerous: the necessity for conversion is not evident to them. And in the end they do not go in to the feast, in the end they remain outside. So we hear the awful words: "You, Capernaum, will you be exalted to heaven? You shall be brought down to Hades. For if the mighty works done in you had been done in Sodom, it would have remained until this day. But I tell you that it shall be more tolerable on the day of judgment for the land of Sodom than for you" (Mt 11,23ff).

The figure of the elder son constrains us to examine our consciences; this figure makes us understand the reinterpretation of the Decalogue found in the Sermon on the Mount: not only outward adultery, but also that inner departure from God; it is possible to remain at home and go away at the same time. Let us understand in that same way also 'abundance', the structure of Christian justice, proof of which is the 'no' to envy, the 'yes' to divine pity, sharing in that mercy by our fraternal compassion.

2. With this observation let us go back to the prayer of the day: "Eternal Father, turn our hearts to you. By seeking your kingdom . . . may we become a people who worship you . . .", or as the original text of the Leonine Sacramentary has it: "Tuo cultui subiectos" (people dedicated to worship you). The primary purpose of the 'return', of conversion, is worship. Conversion is the open space for putting God first. "To prefer nothing to the work of God" — this axiom of St Benedict does not refer only to monks, but should be the rule of life for everyone. Where God is recognised with the whole heart, where God is held in honour, all is well with men and women. What characterises both paradise and the New Jerusalem is God's presence, being with God, living in the light of God's glory, in the light of truth. The original text of the prayer

expresses this order in human life in all clarity: "For they lack nothing, those whom you choose to worship you". These words in the liturgy re-echo Jesus' command: "Seek first the kingdom of God and his righteousness, and all these things shall be yours as well" (Mt 6,33). A rule, this, it seems to me, which is very important in our present-day situation. In view of the enormous poverty of so many countries in the Third World, many, practising Christians even, are thinking today that perhaps it is no longer possible to keep this command-ment; they think that the proclamation of the faith, worship, adoration, should be deferred for a while: first set in order the human problems. But with just such an inversion the problems multiply, the misery grows. God is and remains the primary business of humankind, and where the presence of God is bracketted-out, there is excluded the humanity of human beings, there follows the temptation of the devil in the desert, and in the end people are not saved but destroyed.

The new text of the prayer throws into relief the same truth, but with a different shade of meaning: "Turn our hearts to you. Grant that in our service of you we may follow the example of both Martha and Mary . . .". The primacy of God is underlined by the allusion to the story of Martha and Mary: "One thing is needful" (Lk 10,42). The primacy of the 'one thing', of being with the Lord, listening to his word, the "Seek first the kingdom of God", remains thus the kernel of the text. But with the addition of "performing our deeds of charity" it becomes clear that from his word, from adoration, springs love and work for the renewal of the world.

3. One last observation. According to the tradition of the Church the first week of Lent is the week of Spring Ember Days. Ember Days are specifically a tradition of the Church in Rome, its roots partly to be found in the Old Testament — where for example the prophet Zechariah attests four seasons of fasting in the year — and partly in the tradition of pagan Rome, with its festivals of seedtime and harvest still recalled in our own days. So we have this fine combination of creation and biblical history, a combination which is a sign of true catholicity. In the celebrations of these days we receive the year from the hand of God, receive our time from the Creator

and Redeemer, and confide sowing and harvesting to his goodness, thanking him for the fruit of the earth and our work.
The celebration of the Ember Days corresponds to the fact
that "the creating waits with eager longing for the revealing
of the sons of God" (Rom 8,19): through our prayer, creation
enters into the Eucharist, has part in the praise of God.

In the fifth century however the Ember Days took on another dimension, becoming feasts of the spiritual harvest of
the Church, feasts of Holy Orders. The arrangement of
stational churches for these three days is very significant:
Wednesday, Saint Mary Major; Friday, the Church of the
Twelve Apostles; Saturday, St Peter's. On the first day the
Church presented the ordinands to Our Lady, to the Church
in person. "Sub tuum praesidium confugimus" (We fly to your
protection), a Marian prayer of the third century, comes to
mind here when we meditate on this action. The Church con-
fides her ministers to the Mother: "Behold your mother".
This word from the Cross encourages us to seek refuge close
to our Mother. Under Our Lady's mantle we are safe. In all
our difficulties we can turn with immense faith to our Mother.
What was then done on the Wednesday, Ember Day, has
reference to us: as ministers of the Church we are 'assumed'
into this gesture, the true beginning of our ordination; entrusted to our Mother, we venture to take up our service.

The Friday was the day of the Twelve Apostles' church. As
"fellow-citizens of the saints and servants of God" we
"are built upon the foundation of the apostles and prophets"
(Eph 2,19-20). Only in the context of the apostolic succession,
of the faith of the Apostles and of the apostolic structure of
the Church, with a true priestly system, that is, can we
construct the living temple of God. The ordinations themselves took place during the night of Saturday, with a view
to Sunday morning in St Peter's. Thus the Church expressed
the unity of the priestly system in union with Peter, as
Jesus at the beginning of his public life had called Peter and
his "partners" (Lk 5,10), after he had been teaching from
Simon's boat.

The first week of Lent is a week of seedtime: let us entrust
to God's goodness the fruits of the earth and the work of human
hands, so that all may receive daily bread, so that hunger

may be taken from the earth. Let us entrust to God's goodness also the seed of the word, so as to revive in ourselves the gift of God which is in us "through the laying-on of the hands" of the bishop (2 Tim 1,6), in the apostolic succession, in union with Peter. Let us thank God who has protected us in all temptations and difficulties, and pray, in the words of the prayer after Communion, that God will extend to us his favour, that is, his eternal love, himself, the gift of the Holy Spirit, and that he will grant us also the temporal consolations that we need in our weakness:

> "You have strengthened us Lord, through these mysteries and nourished us with your heavenly sacrament. Stay with us to *comfort us* and *save us*, and *never cease* to show us your *favour*".

Let us make our prayer "through Christ our Lord". Let us pray as under our Mother's mantle. Let us pray as trustful children. The word of the Redeemer stands firm: 'Have faith — I have overcome the world" (Jn 16,33).

Second Sunday of Lent

(Gen 15,5-12.17-18; Phil 3,17-4, 1; Lk 9,26-36)

In this introduction to the Sunday liturgy I wish to present only a brief thought regarding the first Reading of the Sunday: Gen 15,5-12.17-18, a text which at first sight sounds strange to our ears. Note the great distance which separates us from this text in time; the exegetes in fact say that it is a question of a text from a very ancient tradition, bound-up with archaic imagery; this makes all the more surprising the fact that deep down the text outlines the mystery of the crucified Lord.

The event described in the text belongs to the central part of the history of salvation: the conclusion of the pact between God and Abraham has just been recounted. Here, therefore, begins that covenant, that testament from God, which is to have its continuation in Moses and will find its definitive embodiment in Christ. The concluding of the pact is carried out in the forms usual to peoples having no script as yet, and here we find precisely the most sure type of contract for guaranteeing fidelity and security. Two animals are divided into two and the contracting party passes in between the two halves. This action was a risky undertaking because it expressed an obligation which was final and irrevocable, bringing a kind of curse on oneself in the case of breaking the pact, and consequently a binding of one's life and fortune by giving one's word. The action says: the fate of these animals divided in two will be mine if I am not faithful to my word; like these animals I will be cut in pieces should I be unfaithful. The man doing this is saying that he is prepared to give his life for his word, he unites his life to his word which thus becomes his destiny, of higher value than mere biological life. By doing this Abraham *believes*, he entrusts his life to the words of this contract, entrusts his life, irrevocably, to the promise of the covenant. The promise becomes the span of his life, and with his readiness to give his life for his promise, the Patriarch initiates the confessions of the martyrs, recognising the unattainable greatness of God, of truth. Faith is worthy also of suffering. Faith is worthy of a commitment of life until death. To believe means to stake one's life on the word of God; to unite one's life and fate to that word; to be prepared to sacrifice one's standing, to deny oneself any right over oneself and one's time, for the word of God.

In affirming this truth we have interpreted only the more obvious part of the text; there comes now a more obscure aspect and one which is more important. The text says that, when the sun was going down, a deep sleep fell on Abraham; the word used here for a deep sleep is the same word employed in the creation story, when God created the woman from Adam's rib while he was asleep. This word *tardema* gives the meaning of a sleep out of the ordinary, a becoming deaf to all surrounding, everyday things; a dropping down through the levels of being, and reaching that depth where one arrives at the ground of being, touches the ultimate centre of reality — God. At this mysterious depth Abraham sees something strange and stirring: something like a furnace and a blazing torch passing between the halves of the animals. Furnace and fire are representations of the mystery of the invisible God. The furnace and the torch are in reality fire subdued and at the same time dangerous. Thus is expressed the inexpressible mystery of God which is at the same time order, discipline, and supreme power. The representation of God, his mysterious presence, passes between the halves of the animals. This says to us: God too follows the rite of promise, he too stakes his life and his fulness on this covenant; he too will claim to be prepared to give his life for this covenant; he too engages himself and his life to cement irrevocable loyalty to the covenant. At first sight, from a philosophical standpoint, this fact seems simply absurd: how could God suffer, die, bind his fate to the covenant with humankind, with Abraham? The bleeding head, crowned with a wreath of thorns, the crucified Lord, is the answer. The Son of God has borne the curse of the broken promise of the children of Abraham. Thus the unthinkable and the unimaginable is realised: for God, human-

59

kind is so important as to be worthy of his own passion. God offers the price of his fidelity in the incarnate Son, who gives his own life. He accepts to be cut to pieces, to be slain like those animals, when in the final passion of Good Friday the body of the Son will be snatched away from the hand of God and given into the hands of death. God takes humankind seriously — he joins himself in a covenant with them, and in the Holy Eucharist, fruit of the Cross, gives his life into our hands, day after day.

In Abraham's vision, at the very beginning of the covenant with the Chosen People, the first Station of the Cross is already erected. This is, under the veil of mystery, a first vision of the suffering Lord, the crucified God; in images hardly emerged from paganism is expressed the mystery of faith. Abraham's enigmatic vision is reality thrown open to us in the sign of the Cross. With this image the voice of God knocks today at the door of our heart, and the text from the Old Testament expresses none other than the voice of God in the New Testament: "This is my Son, my Chosen; listen to him" (Lk 9,35).

God's faithfulness unto death is in search of our faithfulness. The word of God is very important in our private life. Such a supremacy of the word of God does not apply only to red martyrdom. God's message, which stakes his life on the covenant with us, is a message for everyday life: in the little things, in the patience of faith every day, is realised the way of faithfulness; and so, fixing our eyes on the blood of Christ, we convert ourselves always more and more to his love (cf. First Letter of Clement 7,4).

NOTES

1. Cf. A. De Halleux, *Philoxène de Mabbog*, Louvain 1963 (here quoted according to an allusion in A. Grillmeier, *Philosophie und Theologie*, 55, 1980).
2. For my interpretation of the prayers I have availed myself of J. Pascher's book *Die Orationen des Missale Romanum Papst Paul's VI*.
3. Cf. H. Grisar, *Analecta Romana*, I, Rome 1899; id., *Das Missale im Lichte Römischer Stadtgeschichte*, Freiburg 1925; E. Langer, *Das Stationssystem des 4. Jahrunderts in Jerusalem, Vorbild der Romischen Stationen*, Prague 1900; H. Leclerq, *Stations liturgiques, in* DACL, XV (1953).

4. This meditation corresponds in substance to my homily published in J. Ratzinger & H. U. von Balthasar, *Maria Chiesa nascente*, Rome 1981.

5. Cf. I. de la Potterie, *La mère de Jesus e la concepion virginale du Fils de Dieu*, in *Marianum* 40, 1978.

6. Cf. J. Jeremias, *Ionas*, in *ThWNT* III.

7. Songs of Songs 26,5; PL 183, 906; cf. H. de Lubac, *Histoire et Esprit*, Paris 1950 (ch. 5: Le Dieu d'Origène); J. Ratzinger, *Schauen auf den Durchbohrten*, Einsiedeln 1984.

8. I am practically quoting, here, pp. 206-211 of my *Introduzione al Christianesimo*, Brescia 1974.

9. Pope John Paul II, Encyclical *Dives in misericordia*, IV, 6.

10. I have developed this exegesis of a theme common to the Old and New Testaments in my article 'Fraternité', in *Dictionnaire de spiritualité ascétique et mystique*, V, 1141-1167.

Publisher's note: The prayers for the day, in these meditations, were quoted in the original Latin; here, they are not given in the official translation.

Part II

The Mystery of Jesus

Chapter 1

"He came down from heaven"

1. Questions and first replies

After having confessed the eternal divinity of Jesus, the great ecumenical Creed of the Councils of Nicaea and Constantinople begins its confession of the mystery of the Incarnation with the words: "For us and for our salvation he came down from heaven". If the word so often discussed, 'consubstantialis' (of the same substance), is the key word in the confession of the divinity of Our Lord, the central point of the mystery of the Incarnation is expressed in particular in the word 'descendit'. The Son of God 'comes down'.

The modern mentality finds unsuitable the action expressed in this verb.

I think this must be the reason why, for example, the German translation omits it. But it is exactly in such expressions, in words at first sight not plausible, not acceptable, that the mystery knocks at our hearts. To enter into the mystery, we have to penetrate such words and overcome the first superficial impression of non-acceptability.

Why does this formula appear unsuited? What are the motives for a sort of resistance to accepting it? If we ask ourselves a question such as this, there promptly emerges a primary question: Can God make himself dependent on humankind? Can the contingent be space for the eternal? Can the motive of God's action be other than God himself? Can God operate for a reality which is not himself? Could it be possible that God operates in the divine manner, as God, precisely when he is operating through human beings, his creatures?

A second objection is not so important, but much more tangible: Do we not presuppose here a conception of the world on three levels, in mythological style? Is not this a hypothetical God living on high, up above the clouds, while human beings live down below, and the earth is at the bottom of creation, down to which God has to descend to set everything to rights?

However, there are some problems, even more difficult than the preceding, from several points of view, that remain obscure for us, and yet at the same time provide a solution to the main problems. The idea of someone coming down from above does not suit us. We do not like the word 'condescension': we want parity. The biblical phrase that suits us is "he has put down the mighty from their thrones", much more than "he came down from heaven", although both are valid, in that it is precisely God who both comes down, and who deposes the powerful and raises to the first rank those who until then were last. But we want to bring down the powerful by ourselves, without the God who comes down. The idea of a world in which there is no longer any high and low, the idea of a world of equality in every sense without any fixed point of reference, is not just superficial. It also corresponds to a new attitude in the face of reality which sees high and low as a fraud, and wants to bring lower what is high in the name of equality, liberty and human dignity. In reality we can conclude: if God came down, if now he is low, then low is high. And so the old division into low and high disappears, and our idea of the world and of humankind changes. But it has been changed precisely by that God who has come down.

Therefore, first of all, the irreplaceable statement remains: he *has* come down. And this means: the highness, the majesty, the lordship of God and of Jesus Christ *exist*: the absolute majesty of his word, of his love, of his power. What is 'high' does exist — God; the second article of the Creed does not cancel out the first. Even in his lowest descent, even in the most extreme abasement and hiddenness, God remains what is truly high. At the very beginning of the history of salvation the declaration "God is" is powerfully brought out. First we have to recall the intangible majesty of him from whom everything is; if this is not perceived, then the descent of God too is robbed of its greatness and is lost in the general monotone, the vague fluctuations of what is always equal. If it is not perceived, the drama of human history loses all the interplay of its tensions and its meaning. Not only that; human-kind itself does not increase in dignity, but on the contrary it diminishes; certainly it is no longer 'high' in the world but one of its freaks, an unfinished experiment, "the animal which is still undefined" (Nietzsche).

Anyone wanting to understand this descent must have first understood the mystery of the 'on high' which we convey by the word 'heaven'.

To begin with, there is the mystery of the burning bush: the power which constrains us to fear, establishes its criteria. But the fire of the burning bush is no earthly fire in the sense of the stoic philosophers: from it issues a voice; by this fire is manifested that God has heard the complaint of Israel, the cry for help of those who have been enslaved. This fire is also God already come down to rescue the perishing. We can there-fore now say as the first consequence of this consideration, that while there is no descent geographically speaking from an upper level of the universe to a lower, there yet exists some-thing much more profound, which has to be symbolised by cosmic images: the advent of God's essence into the human essence, and, still more, the way from lordship to the Cross, the coming for the sake of those who are last, who, precisely in virtue of this become the first.

2. A biblical interpretation of the descent of the Son

The depth of meaning inherent in the word 'descent' can certainly be understood, in a kind of way, by following the long history of this word through the writings of the Old and New Testaments, from which rises a rivulet which then, gathering brooks and tributaries, becomes an ever greater stream. In the account of the building of the Tower of Babel we first meet the 'descent' of God, a coming down in wrath, to which the story of the burning bush appears by contrast as a new descent in compassion and love. In the space of this Retreat we cannot follow the whole history; let us consider only a passage from chapter 10 of the Letter to the Hebrews in which we find one of the most profound interpretations of the descent of the Son, with no suggestion of spacial connota-tion, and in which light is thrown fully on the spiritual and personal content of the word. The author of the Letter takes up once again his fundamental theme that the offering of animals is not capable of re-establishing relations between humankind and God, and continues: "Consequently, when Christ came into the world, he said: sacrifices and burnt offerings thou hast not desired, but a body hast thou prepared for me; in burnt offerings and sin offerings thou hast taken no pleasure. Then I said, 'Lo, I have come to do thy will, O God', as it is written of me in the book" (Heb 10,5-7; cf. Ps 40,7-8).

By use of the words of a Psalm which is presented as an entrance chant for the coming of Christ into the world, the Letter gives here a true and fitting theology of the incarnation in which there are no references on the cosmic level: the 'coming down', the 'coming into', are interpreted rather as a process of prayer; prayer is then certainly intended as a preliminary to a journey, as an involvement of the whole being, setting off in prayer, freeing itself from itself, sublimating itself. The entry of Christ into the cosmos is categorised here as a willed and responsible event, as the real fulfilment of a line of thought and faith expressed in many of the Psalms.

Let us now examine more closely the text of the Psalm and its New Testament transmutation. What is this Psalm saying? It is the thanksgiving of someone God has awakened from death. But the person praying is thanking God, now, in terms of what he holds to be true piety, and not by means of animal sacrifices; in line with prophetic tradition he knows that: "sacrifices and offerings thou dost not desire; but thou hast given me an open ear" (v. 6). This means: God does not want anything else from us but that we listen — that we remain listening, that we obey — and, through this our availability, we give our very self. The psalmist's expression of gratitude to God, in compliance with the true God, is: to do God's will. This process of listening and responding is the sacrifice pleasing to God.

For the Letter to the Hebrews these words of the Psalm are part of that dialogue between the Father and the Son which is the Incarnation. In this Letter the Incarnation becomes perceptible as the inherently trinitarian spiritual process. In the light of the Prophecy the Letter to the Hebrews has changed only one word of the Psalm: in the place of 'ear', hearing, is substituted the word 'body' — "A body hast thou prepared for me". By the word 'body' is meant here humankind itself, the human being. Obedience becomes incarnate; in its fullest expression it is no longer simply hearing but becoming flesh. The theology of the word becomes theology of the Incarnation. The surrender of the Son to the Father emerges from the divine dialogue and becomes acceptance of the human being; and therefore the surrender of all creation to the Father is summed up in man. This body, or better Jesus' humanity, is the outcome of obedience, the fruit of the responsive love of the Son; and at the same time it is prayer become concrete. The humanity of Jesus is in this sense already an entirely spiritual fact, 'divine' from its very origin.

If we meditate on this, it becomes clear that the abasement of the Incarnation, or rather the descent from the Cross, is in profound inner correspondence with the mystery of the Son: the Son by his essence is the gift and giving back of himself: this is what is meant by 'being son'. The Incarnation of the Son means from the beginning: "he became obedient unto death" (Phil 2,8). But then the text is again turned towards us, at the height of the mystery: we are in the image of God not when we set ourselves up as self-sufficient, not when we seek an autonomy without any barriers. Attempts of this kind encounter an inner contradiction, are ultimately a lie. We become God by sharing in the action of the Son. We become God in the measure that we become 'children', make ourselves 'offspring': which means we become so when we enter into the dialogue of Jesus with his Father and when this dialogue with our Father is enfleshed in the composition of our daily life: "A body hast thou prepared for me. . .". Our salvation consists in becoming the 'body of Christ', like to Christ himself; in accepting ourselves every day from him; in giving back every day, offering every day our body as place for the word. This we become when we follow him, in descending and ascending. All this is contained in the simple phrase "he came down from heaven". It speaks of Christ, and precisely in him is speaking of us. The whole of this confession is not exhausted in one interchange. It is needs to go from word to body, from body to word; only in passing from word to body and from body to word can it be really made our own.

Chapter 2

"And he was made man"

The words of St John on the Incarnation of God in Jesus is the heart of our Christological confession: the real, the divine interpretation of the descent of the Son. These words are consequently the starting point and reference for all theological work on Christology. Here, in our journey of preparation for the Paschal Mystery, we are not going to consider the conceptual constructions of the theologians, but rather the mysteries of the life of Jesus. Contemplative prayer, followed by meditative painting, used to immerse itself lovingly in the various phases of the itinerary in the earthly life of Jesus, to see as near as one could that infinite gulf which opens up when we say "The Son of God was made man".

Besides the metaphysical understanding of these words, there always remains a need for that other attempt at an approach: meditation on the images of the life of Jesus and on his concrete earthly existence that cannot be reduced to the supra-temporal mould of abstract concepts. Always necessary is the heart's vision in order to follow the various revelations of the divine and human mystery in the various fundamental stages of the life, in its various events, and in the acting and suffering of Jesus. Let us single out three aspects: his infancy, his adult life and his death.

1. The theological significance of the infancy of Jesus

By becoming incarnate, Jesus became a baby. 'To *become* man', and to appear in the form of a man, means to accept that humble road which begins in infancy and in the humility of conception in the womb of the mother. To be human implies: becoming a baby. What does 'being a baby', 'being a child' mean? It is dependency in absolutely everything; needing help, having to turn to others. As a baby, Jesus comes not only from God but also from other humans. He has been in the womb of a woman, from whom he received his flesh and his blood, the beating of his heart, his bearing, his words.

He has received life from the life of another human being. A derivation like this, from others, of what is proper to oneself is not a purely biological factor. It means that Jesus received also his manner of thinking and observing, the cast of his human soul, from people existing before him, and finally from his mother. It means that in what he inherited from his ancestors he wanted to follow the tortuous road leading back from Mary to Abraham and finally to Adam. He carried in himself the burden of that history; he lived and suffered it, purging it of all the refuse and error, for it to become a pure 'Yes': "For the Son of God, Jesus Christ, was not Yes and No; but in him it is always Yes" (2 Cor 1,19).

It is surprising, the eminence which Jesus himself conferred on being a child: 'Truly, I say to you, unless you turn and become like children, you will never enter the kingdom of heaven" (Mt 18,3). To be a child, then, is not for Jesus a purely transitory period in anyone's life — biological, and therefore to be completely cancelled out later on; in infancy, what is proper to a human being is realised in such a way that one who has missed childhood has missed him or herself. From this, identifying with the human aspect, we can imagine what happy memories Jesus must have had of the days of his childhood, how it must have remained for him a precious experience, a particularly pure form of human life. From this we can learn to have reverence for the child, who precisely by its want of defences calls for our love. But the question that arises above all else is: Exactly what is characteristic about being a child, that Jesus considers so indispensable? It is in fact clear that it is not a matter here of a romantic idealisation of little ones, nor of a moral judgment, but of some more profound connotation.

We must first of all consider how the central designation of Jesus, the one which expresses his dignity, is that of 'Son'. To answer the question in what measure this designation already figured orally in the actual historical words of Jesus, we might ordinarily say that it undoubtedly constitutes an attempt to resume in one word the total impression of his life. The orientation of his life, the original motive and the aim which shaped it are expressed in one word: Abba — beloved Father. Jesus knew himself to be never alone, and to the very end, at the final cry from the Cross, he followed him whom he called Father, he was entirely directed towards him. Only so is it possible that he wanted to be called not king, nor lord, nor by any name attributing power, but by a word which we could also translate as 'child'. We could then go on to say: infancy assumes an almost extraordinary place in Jesus' preaching because of its being what corresponds most profoundly to his most personal mystery, his Sonship. His highest dignity, referring back to his divinity, is, after all, not power possessed by himself; it is based on the fact of his being turned towards the Other — God the Father. The German exegete Joachim Jeremias puts it very well when he says that to be children in Jesus' sense means to learn to say 'Father'.[1] But only if we look at it seeing Jesus as Son, can we estimate the immense power which resides in this word. Human beings want to become God and — given a proper interpretation of the term — should become so. But when, as in the immortal interchange with the serpent in the earthly paradise, humankind seeks to attain to it by freeing itself from God and its creaturely status, setting itself up and centering on itself, when, in a word, it becomes completely grown up and emancipated, casting off childhood entirely as a mode of being, then it ends up as nothing, because it is setting itself against the truth of its being, which is to refer everything to God. It is only by preserving the innermost heart of infancy, the existence, that is, of Son as lived by Jesus, that humanity enters with the Son into divinity.

Another aspect of what Jesus means by our 'being children' comes out clearly when he extols the poor: "Blessed are you poor, for yours is the kingdom of God" (Lk 6,20).

In this passage the poor have replaced the children. Once again, it is not a question of romanticising poverty or of moral judgments about individuals, poor or rich, but of what is most profound in human nature. From what is said of being poor,

72

therefore, it becomes sufficiently clear what is meant by being children: the child possesses nothing of itself, it receives all it needs for life from others; the child is free: it does not make any attempt to hide what it really is. Possession and power are humankind's two great shackles by which we become imprisoned, through having and through giving our hearts to these things. Anyone who, by having, is not able to remain poor at heart and to recognise that the world is in God's hands and not in ours, will have lost that childlikeness without which we cannot enter the Kingdom. The Greek Metropolitan Stylianos Harkianakis recalls in this regard that Plato in his *Timeon* spoke of the ironical judgment of a non-Greek who affirmed that the Greeks were *aei paides*, eternal children. Plato does not see any reproach in this, but a tribute to the Greek character. "It remains firmly accepted that the Greeks want to be a people of philosophers and not technocrats, that is, eternal children, apt to wonder in amazement at the higher states of human existence. Only in this light can we view the important fact that the Greeks have made no practical use of their innumerable inventions".[2]

In this suggestion of the latent affinity between the Greek mind and the message of the Gospel there is also an echo of something which concerns us here: wonder should not be lost — the capacity, that is, to marvel and to listen, to ask not only about what is functional but equally to perceive the harmony of the spheres and to rejoice precisely that it is of no obvious use to us.

We want to go on a stage further. To be children means saying 'Father', as we have seen. Now we must add: to be children means saying 'Mother'. If we remove this possibility we eliminate in fact the human element from the childhood of Jesus, leaving only the Sonship of the Word, which is revealed to us precisely by the *human* childhood of Jesus. Hans Urs von Balthasar has formulated this concept admirably; so it is worth our while to quote him at length. "*Eucharistia* means rendering thanks: how wonderful that Jesus gives thanks, by offering himself and giving himself without end to God and to human beings. Who is it he is thanking? Certainly he is thanking God the Father, prototype and source of every gift. . . But he thanks also the poor sinners who have willingly received him,

who have let him enter under their unworthy roof. Does he
also thank anyone else? I think so: he thanks the humble
maiden from whom he received this flesh and this blood when
the Holy Spirit overshadowed her. . . What does Jesus learn
from his mother? He learns her 'yes'. Not any yes, but the
'yes' which goes on always without wearying. Everything you
ask, my God. . . 'Behold the handmaid of the Lord. Be it
done unto me according to your word". . . This is the catholic
prayer that Jesus learnt from his earthly mother, from Mater
Catholica, who was in the world before him and was inspired
by God to be the first to pronounce these words of the new
and eternal covenant. . .".[3]

In Stylianos Harkianakis is to be found moreover an observation according to which the logic of the child has assumed a
character so plain and convincing that any rational explanation
could be only a pale abstraction before it, deprived of the
splendour of childlike contemplation: 'A monk of the monastery of Iviron on Mt Athos said to me once: We honour the
Mother of God and we have put all our hope in her because
we know she can do everything. And do you know why she
can do everything? Her Son does not refuse anything she
wishes, because he has not been able to give back to her what
he took on loan from her. He took his flesh from her, and
made it divine, but he did not give it back. This is why we
feel ourselves so safe in the garden of the Mother of God".[4]

2. Nazareth

The name of Nazareth has been vitiated for us by the senti-
mental transposition of the life of Jesus into an idyll of a
small middle class. We today reject that view of it as tending
to minimise the mystery. The origin of the devotion to the
Holy Family, which for the most part rises above such a false
interpretation, was certainly something different. It was
developed by Cardinal Laval in Canada in the seventeenth
century, as a call to the responsibility proper to the laity. The
Cardinal "recognised, then, the necessity of giving to the
colonial population a solid social structure, to prevent them
going astray in the absence of traditions and roots. There were

not enough priests to create proper Eucharistic communities. . . He turned all his attention to the family: he entrusted the prayer life to the head of the family. By meditating on the life of Jesus at Nazareth the family was seen as being Church, and the priestly responsibility of the head of the family was discovered".[5]

Jesus grew up a Jew in 'Galilee of the Gentiles', learning the Scriptures, without going to school, in that house where the Word of God dwelt. The few details given in Luke are nonetheless sufficient to give an idea of the spirit which marked this family community in which the true Israel came to its realisation. Especially we recognise from the masterly way Jesus reads the Scriptures, his confident knowledge of them, and his command of the rabbinical tradition, how much he learned from their time together in Nazareth.

And has all this no importance for us, in an age when Christians for the most part have to live in a 'Galilee of the Gentiles'? The Church cannot grow and prosper if she is not aware that her hidden roots are in the atmosphere of Nazareth.

Yet another point of view calls for our attention. In the midst of the flourishing of that stylised Nazareth, the true mystery of Nazareth, unnoticed by contemporaries, has been rediscovered and at its greatest depth. It was for Charles de Foucauld to discover Nazareth in his search for 'the lowest place'. During his Holy Land pilgrimage it was this locality which influenced him the most; he did not feel himself called "to follow Christ in the public life, but Nazareth affected him to the depths of his heart". He wanted to follow the Jesus who is silent, the Jesus who is poor, the Jesus who labours. He wanted to fulfil literally that saying of Jesus: "When you are invited to the marriage feast, go and sit in the lowest place" (Lk 14,10). He knew that Jesus himself had expounded this saying by his own example; he knew that even before dying on the Cross naked and without any possession he had made his definitive choice — 'the lowest place' — while at Nazareth. Charles de Foucauld found his own Nazareth first among the Trappists of Notre Dame des Neiges (in 1890) and six months later in the Trappist monastery of Akbes in Syria still poorer than that, subsequently, of Notre Dame du Sacré Coeur. From here he wrote to his sister: "Let us do the work of peasants, work infinitely salutary for the soul, in doing which it is possible to meditate and pray. . . We come to understand so well what a piece of bread means when we know from personal experience how much fatigue it costs to produce it. . .".[6]

In his pilgrimage on the track of the 'mystery of the life of Jesus' Charles de Foucauld found Jesus the worker. He encountered the real 'historical Jesus'. While he was working at Notre Dame du Sacré Coeur, in 1892, Martin Kühler's seminal book entitled *The So-called Historical Jesus and the Christ of Biblical History* appeared in Europe. It first brought to a head the polemic on the historical Jesus. Later it became the starting point for the reflections of R. Bultmann on *The Historical Jesus*. The Brother in the Syrian Trappist monastery knew nothing of this, but entering into the Nazareth experience of Jesus taught him more than could have been brought to light in any learned discussion. So, through living meditation on Jesus, a new contemporary way of life came to be opened for the Church. In fact, to work with Jesus the worker, to plunge oneself into 'Nazareth', became the starting point for a new idea of the Church, poor and humble, a family-Church, a Nazareth Church.

Nazareth has a permanent message for the Church. The New Covenant did not begin in the Temple, nor on the Holy Mount, but in the Virgin's humble dwelling, in a worker's home, in an out of the way place in 'Galilee of the Gentiles', from which no one expected any good to come. The Church has always to start again from here, begin healing from here. She cannot give the right response to the revolt of our century against the power of riches if Nazareth does not remain in her as a lived reality.

3. The public life and the hidden life

After the time of silence, of learning, of waiting, follows the work, the coming out into the public eye. The humanity of Jesus also means: sharing in the joy and success which public life has to offer, and sharing in the joy of humankind's work which leads to success. It certainly also means: sharing in the burden and the responsibility consequent on public life. People in public life do not acquire friends only but are exposed also to opposition, incomprehension, and abuse. Their name and their words can be used, now by the left, now by the right. Antichrist masks himself as Jesus; he will make use of him as the devil makes use of God's word, the Bible (Mt 4,1-11; Lk 4,1-13). Paradoxically, public life also means loneliness. So it happens for Jesus too: he gathers friends, but he is not spared the delusion of a betrayal of friendship, as he is not spared either the incomprehension of well-intentioned disciples, weak none the less. At the end there is the loneliness of that hour of anguish on the Mount of Olives, when the disciples sleep: in his most intimate self, he is not understood.

Besides the loneliness of incomprehension there is still another kind of loneliness, the uniqueness of Jesus. He has lived his life from a standpoint to which others cannot penetrate, that of being alone with God. About him, that saying of William of St Thierry has total meaning and in a way more profound than for others: "One who is with God is not less alone than when alone".

In saying this we touch on the heart of the Christological mystery. The Christological faith of the Church starts out from meditation on the prayer of Jesus. Prayer is his hidden life and the key to his public life. Our next meditation must therefore centre on this fundamental reality: the prayer of Jesus.

Chapter 3

"True God and true man"

1. Prayer — centre and keynote of the life of Jesus

A decisive moment in the history of Jesus and of the Church then being founded was that described in the Gospel for today, the feast of St Peter's Chair: the moment when Jesus — already excluded from the Synagogue — asked his disciples: "Who do men say that I am? And who do you say that I am?" (Mk 8,27ff). In that hour the confession of Christological faith began, and with the confession in common began the life of the Church. Jesus' question is repeated in every generation: "Who do men say that I am? And who do you say that I am?" It is the central question of our lives and of this Retreat.

The answer the people gave and Peter's answer differently reflect the attempt to find categories for delineating the figure of Jesus. Although other people's replies express some part of the truth, Peter's alone hits the mark and thus becomes the nucleus of what will later be developed into the Credo of the Church — that Credo which, to start with, is the Petrine Creed. Peter's reply, in its first formulation transmitted by St Mark, is the nucleus, but only the nucleus, the germ of the Church's Creed: "You are the Christ [the Messiah]" (v. 28). This formula expresses the essential, but it could not suffice of itself because of the many meanings of the title Messiah. This ambiguity shows itself immediately after the confession, when Peter feels constrained to reprove Jesus on account of his foretelling of the Cross, so that Jesus must say: "Get behind me, Satan! For you are not on the side of God but of men" (Mk 8,33).

The versions of Peter's confession presented in the Gospels of Luke and Matthew point the way to the deepening and clarification of the first formula; they reflect the path of faith of Peter and of the nascent Church — the first and decisive stage of the history of dogma. This biblical account of Peter's confession was the crystallising point of faith in Jesus the Christ, but at the same time there remained open a wider area of possible complementary interpretations which are reflected in an abundance of other titles such as: prophet, priest, paraclete, angel, lord, son of God, Son. The primitive Church's striving after the right understanding of Christ appears to us as in reality a process in which faith is seeking order: the relationship of the titles to one another, a sifting of them so as to arrive at a greater simplification and concentration. Finally, there remained three titles as a general and valid description of the mystery of Jesus: Christ — Lord — Son (of God).

Since the title Christ (Messiah) increasingly combined with the name Jesus and yet as regards its content had not a clear meaning to those outside the Jewish world, and also because the form 'Lord' in contemporary language remained ambiguous, a final process of concentration and simplification was necessary. The single title 'Son' showed itelf in the end to be the sole comprehensive description for all, and sufficient moreover to express the content of all the other titles. The word 'Son' contains all the rest and at the same time explains the rest. The Church's profession of faith could therefore in the end settle for this title, which we find in its definitive form in Matthew with Peter's profession of faith: "You are the Christ, the Son of the living God" (Mt 16,16).

While however the Church has concentrated in this one word the structure of a tradition which is so diverse, giving at the same time a final simplification to the fundamental Christian definition, it should not for all that be considered as a simplification in the simplist, reductionist sense; in the term 'Son' is to be found that simplicity which is at the same time profundity and amplitude. 'Son', as a fundamental profession of faith, signifies that in this term is given the key interpretation which makes all the rest accessible and understandable.

At this point we encounter the whole business of the modern discussion on Jesus — a discussion which is fundamentally a return to the opinions of people who did not know Jesus. The arguments are seductive. It is said that such a concentration of inherited history is a falsification of the sources, especially by the fact that the historical distance appears too great.

Before replying to this argument I should like to insist once again on the simplicity of the dogma as regards biblical tradition. Many think that Church dogma has obscured the simplicity of the Gospel with an impenetrable mass of philosophical concepts, and so made inaccessible the Jesus of the Bible. The contrary is true: the history of Christological dogma is a process of simplification and concentration. This process has made a clearance at the centre, combining all the experiences reported and interpreted in the New Testament in this single word 'Son', and has thus provided the hermeneutical key which opens the door to the depths of the person and history of Jesus.

But let us return to our starting point. Is this concentration perhaps a falsification?

In reality the Church has responded, with this interpretation of the figure of Jesus, to the fundamental *historical* experience of him which eye witnesses had made of him during his life. To call Jesus the 'Son' does not in fact mean to apply to him the mythical gold of dogma (as has been affirmed again after Reimarus); it corresponds instead in more terse fashion to the centrality of the historical figure of Jesus. In this phrase is concentrated the experience of the 'you' — in contrast to 'people' — who knew Jesus intimately. The whole of the Gospel testimony is unanimous, in fact, in bringing out those words and actions of Jesus which flowed from his intimate communion of life with the Father; that he, after the fatigues of the day, always went up "into a mountain" to pray alone (cf. for example Mk 1,35; 6,46; 14,35-39). According to the unanimous and incontestable witness of the Gospels the following thesis can be formulated: the life and person of Jesus centred on his constant communication with the Father. Of the Evangelists Luke is the first to underline forcefully this behaviour as factual. He demonstrates that the solid results of Jesus' work sprang from the centre of his person, and this centre was his intercourse with the Father. I will cite three examples:

1. Let us begin with the calling of the Twelve, their symbolic number expressing a reference to the new people of God of

which they were destined to become the pillars. With them, then, by means of a gesture at once symbolic and completely real, Jesus initiated the 'People of God'; so this means that their call is to be considered theologically as the beginning of the 'Church'. According to Luke, Jesus had spent the night preceding this event on the mountain in prayer: the call emanates from prayer, from the intercourse of the Son with the Father. The Church is born in the prayer in which Jesus again commits himself to the Father and the Father delivers everything to the Son. In this most profound communication between Father and Son lies concealed the true and ever new origin of the Church and its secure foundation (Lk 6,12-17).

2. As a second example I propose the account of the origin of the profession of faith in Christ which a short while ago we mentioned already as the central source of the oldest history of Christian dogma. Jesus first asks the Apostles who the Son of Man is in the opinion of the people, and then, who he is according to theirs. To this question, as we know, Peter replies with that confession of faith which continues to build up the Church in communion with Peter. The Church lives by this profession of faith; in it is disclosed to her, with the mystery of Jesus, the mystery of human life, and of the history of human-kind and of the world, because in it is disclosed the mystery of God. This profession of faith unifies the Church; the Simon who makes the profession of faith therefore is to be called Peter, chosen and called to be the rock of unity: profession of faith and Peter's ministry, profession of faith in Jesus Christ and unity of the Church with and around Peter — they are in-divisibly bound together.

Thus we may say that Peter's profession of faith represents the second step in the making of the Church. But also at this point Luke shows that Jesus puts the decisive question to the Apostles about their opinion compared with that of others, precisely at the moment when they had begun to share in the secret of his prayer. Thus the Evangelist makes clear that Peter understands and proclaims the reality of the person of Jesus at the very moment in which, being in prayer, Jesus is aware of his being one with the Father. According to Luke, therefore, it can be seen who Jesus is, if he is seen at prayer. Christian faith derives from sharing in the prayer of Jesus, from involving ourselves with him, being able to penetrate into his prayer; this is interpreting Jesus' experience of prayer and therefore it understands Jesus truly because it derives from sharing in intimacy with him at the heart of his person. We have reached the deepest root and the enduring premise of the Christian faith: only by entering into Christ's solitude, only by *sharing* in his reality, in his communication with the Father, can we *see* this reality of his. Only so can we penetrate to his identity, only so can we begin to understand him and grasp what it means 'to follow Jesus'. Profession of faith in Christ is not an empty phrase; it is prayer and is born only of prayer. The one who has seen Jesus' intimacy with his Father, and from this has understood his reality, is to be called to be the 'rock' of the Church. The Church springs from sharing in the prayer of Jesus (cf. Lk 9,18-20; Mt 16,13-20).

3. For my third example I shall take the episode of the Transfiguration of Jesus 'on the mount'. In the Gospel tradition 'the mount' is always the place of prayer, of being with the Father. On this occasion Jesus had taken with him to the mountain the three who represented the central nucleus of the community of the Twelve: Peter, James and John. "And as he was praying, the appearance of his countenance was altered", recounts Luke (Lk 9,29). By this means he makes clear that the Transfiguration only renders visible what really happens in Jesus' prayer: a sharing in the splendour of God and so a manifestation of the true significance of the Old Testament and the whole of history, that is, revelation. From this sharing in the splendour of God, in the majesty of God, which means at the same time a seeing with God's eye, and therefore a revelation of what is hidden, derives the proclamation of Jesus. With this, Luke indicates at the same time the unity between revelation and prayer in the person of Jesus: the one and the other spring from the mystery of the Sonship. Moreover, according to the Evangelists, the Transfiguration is a kind of anticipation of the Resurrection and of the parousia (cf. Mk 9,1). In fact his communication with the Father, which becomes visible during the prayer of the Transfiguration, is the true reason why Jesus could not remain in death, and why all history is in his hands.

He to whom the Father speaks the word is the Son (cf. Jn 10,33-36). But the Son does not die. Thus Luke points out that the whole of the discussion concerning Christ — Christology — is nothing other than interpreting his prayer: the whole person of Jesus is contained in his prayer.

4. Many proofs in favour of this view can also be deduced from the other Evangelists. I should like to touch briefly on three examples only.

a) My first is the prayer of Jesus in the Garden of Olives which has now — at the time of the beginning of the Passion — become 'the mount' of his being alone with the Father. The use of the name 'Abba' for God, which in this context Mark has transmitted to us from Jesus' mother tongue, Aramaic, surpasses every mode of prayer known at the time; it expresses a kind of familiarity with God which in the Jewish tradition would have appeared impossible and inadmissible. Thus in this one word alone is expressed the singular new mode of relationship of Jesus to God, that relationship for which the denomination 'Son' is the sole expression possible.

b) With this, we are already at the second point which I wish to touch on here, and it is precisely the important use of the words 'Father' and 'Son' which can be observed in the language of Jesus. He never attributed to the Apostles or other persons the name of 'son' or 'sons' as he did to himself. In the same way, he always clearly abstracted the phrase 'my Father' from the sense of the common paternity of God, which holds for all people. The expression 'our Father' is kept for the Apostles, who pray with the 'we' of the apostolic community; this expresses the sharing of his own in the relationship of Jesus with God, which is embodied in the prayer of the Apostles without, for all that, taking away the difference of the mode of relationship with God. In all Jesus' words and actions, this relationship of Son shines out, always present and always effective; it can be seen how his whole being is taken up in this relationship.

c) This 'being-relationship', which is in reality the very person of Jesus, is to be found not only in the various forms in which the word 'Son' appears but also in a series of other expressions which recur in Jesus' message, as for example: "For this am I come"; "For this I have been sent". In accordance with the consciousness of himself, proper to Jesus, as it is revealed in the Gospels, he speaks and acts not of himself but by the working of another, from whom he comes. His whole existence is 'mission', relationship.

If we consider these observations in relation to the synoptic Gospels it becomes intelligible also that the fourth Gospel, which is entirely made up of concepts such as 'Father', 'Son', 'mission', adds nothing substantially foreign to the tradition, but merely underlines more vigorously what the other Evangelists have made known. It could be said the fourth Gospel introduces us into that intimacy with Jesus to which he admits only his friends. This shows Jesus from the point of view of that experience of friendship which allows of seeing into another intimately, and is an invitation to enter, with the disciple whom Jesus loved, into that intimacy which permits us to know Jesus and find in the Saviour the way, the truth and the life.

2. The consonance between the testimony of the Scriptures and Christological dogma

In the preceding conference we limited ourselves to the testimony of the Gospels concerning Jesus. What we found was that the definitive title of the faith for Jesus — Son — corresponds exactly to the historical image of him recognisable in the texts: the centre of his life was his permanent contact with his Father, the intimacy of his prayer. The Christology expressed in the title 'Son' is ultimately a theology of prayer, a concentration of the witnesses' experience with the person of Jesus.

In this conference let us take a step further, proceeding in the Christology of the dogma, that of the great Councils of the Church, Nicaea, Chalcedon, Constantinople. The key word of these Councils is the *omooùsios* (of the same substance), already included in the Symbol of 335 at the Ecumenical Council of Nicaea. In this word the Council Fathers express their synthesis of Hebrew and Greek thought, salvation history, and ontology. My thesis is that what has been said of the concentration of different biblical titles in the word 'Son' is equally valid for this synthesis. Again, this new word is, in the final analysis, nothing other than an interpretation of the life and death of Jesus, which were continuously determined by the intercourse of the Son with the Father. Therefore, as dogmatic and biblical Christology cannot be divided nor opposed, neither can Christology and soteriology. In the same way, 'high' and 'low' Christology, the theology of the Incarnation and the theology of the Cross, form an inseparable whole. Or, in other words: the central term of the dogma 'consubstantial Son', in which is resumed all the testimony of the ancient Councils, simply translates the fact of the prayer of Jesus into philosophical and theological language, and that is all.

To this is now opposed the widespread thesis according to which Scripture and dogma result from two different cultures: Scripture from Hebrew culture and dogma from Greek culture. The transfer of the biblical witness into Greek thought — so it is said — has become at the same time a complete refashioning of the content of the witness concerning Jesus. The faith, which at first was a simple act of trust in salvific grace, would have been thereby transformed into an adherence to certain philosophical paradoxes, into a belief in a determined doctrine. Faith in God's action would be thus substituted for by an ontological doctrine entirely unknown to Scripture.

At this point we should introduce a simple but fundamental human question. The entire Christological discussion treats, in a definite way, of salvation, of the liberation of humankind. But what is it that frees humankind? Who frees and to what end? Or again more simply: What is this 'liberty of humankind'? Can human beings become free apart from the truth, that is, in falsehood, uncertainty, error? A liberation abstracted from the truth, without truth would not be liberation, but rather deception and slavery, the ruin of humankind. Liberty without truth cannot be true liberty — therefore without truth there is no liberty worthy of the name.

Let us add yet another reflection. The human person, to be free, has to be 'like God'. The intention of becoming like God is the central nucleus of so much that is devised about the liberation of humankind. Because the desire of liberty belongs to the essence of a human being, such a person necessarily seeks from the start the path to 'being like God': all other things in fact are not sufficient for human beings, insatiable where finite things are concerned. Our time in particular demonstrates this, with its passionate cry for total freedom and anarchy in face of the insufficiency of all bourgeois freedom, however broad it may be, and for all libertinism. Consequently, an anthropology of liberation, if it wants to correspond to the depth of the problem this raises, cannot avoid the query: How is this end of 'becoming like God', being divinised, to be achieved?

What do we find if we now combine our two reflections? If humankind asks the most necessary questions, inevitable ones indeed — that is, questions on truth and liberty — ontological questions arise. The ontological question in modern theologies, often voiced ironically, has no other motivation than the thirst for liberty, inseparably connected with the want of truth connatural to humankind.

It cannot be said, then, that the problem of being belongs only to a particular stage of spiritual development in humankind, the metaphysical period, the one Auguste Comte, in his 'law of the three stages', locates as the phase midway between the mythological period and the positive; in the second of which, according to him, we should be today and in which the earlier metaphysical problem would be overcome. It is indisputable that the human sciences, which seek to describe humankind 'positively' in the sense of the present-day scientific method, can make important contributions to human knowledge. But in contrast to this, the question of the truth proper to humankind does not, however, become superfluous. It is the question of where the reality which is humankind comes from and for what it is destined. Whenever the human sciences seek to render superfluous the truth of humankind, they become a method of self-alienation and, therefore, of the enslavement of humankind. But the enquiry into freedom, and freedom as a problem of being, includes also an enquiry about God, the problem of God. Thus it is quite certainly possible to catalogue the theological methods of the Fathers of a particular age, and thereby show the limits of their theology; but the questions which that theology raised are necessary questions for humankind always and everywhere. A view of the New Testament which left these questions aside would depart from the essential, and become a marginal abridgement.

With these remarks, let us turn again to the actual point of our question. At first sight it can appear very circumstantial, and purely internal to Christianity, to speak of Jesus' prayer as a fundamenal expression of the New Testament about him. In reality it treats precisely of the point with which we are occupied, humanity's inner core. In fact the New Testament means to indicate by this the setting where human beings can become God: the place, then, of their liberation, the place where they attain freedom and become true.

When we speak of the relationship of Jesus, the Son, with the Father, we touch on a very sensitive point in the problem of the freedom of human beings and their liberation, and without it all the rest comes to nothing. A liberation of humankind without transformation in God would be to deceive human beings and the human desire of the infinite.

Let us add a further note on the language of dogma. The Council of Nicaea, as we know, went beyond the language of the Bible in its Symbol, where it refers to Jesus as "of one substance with the Father". This philosophical term inserted into the Creed — 'consubstantial' — has been notably disputed, in ancient times and in modern. It is always supposed to present a fundamental deviation, not from the language only but also from the thought. Now, this kind of problem can be resolved whenever terms are precisely defined. What does 'consubstantial' really mean? The reply is as follows: This word in its objective intention is none other than the translation into philosophical language of the word 'Son'. But why have this translation? Now, when faith begins to meditate, the question always arises as to what reality can the word 'Son' express in reference to Jesus. Certainly it is a term which is quite usual in religious language, and so one inevitably asks oneself: How is the term 'Son' thought of in this case? Is it a metaphor, as it is ordinarily used in the history of religion, or does it signify something more? If the Council of Nicaea has interpreted the word 'Son' in philosophical fashion, using the term 'consubstantial', it thus signifies that the word 'Son' should not be understood there in the sense of figurative religious language, but in the full meaning of the word. The central word of the New Testament, the term 'Son', is to be understood in a literal sense.

This means that the philosophical term 'consubstantial' adds nothing to the New Testament, but as a defining witness it is the defence of the literal usage against any allegorising. This means then: the word of God does not deceive. Jesus does not merely come to be *called* Son of God, but he *is* so in reality. God does not remain eternally wrapped in the clouds of imagery which screen rather than reveal him. He really comes into touch with human beings and lets them really come into touch with him, in him who is his Son. When the New Testament speaks of the Son, it throws down the dividing wall of imagery in the history of religion and shows us the reality, that is, the truth by which we can live and die. Thus it can be said that it is precisely this learned term 'consubstantial' which defends that simplicity of which the Lord speaks when he says: "I thank thee, Father, Lord of heaven and earth, that thou hast hidden these things from the wise and understanding and revealed them to babes" (Mt 11,25; cf. 1 Pet 2,2).

But the development of dogmatic theology did not end with the Councils of Nicaea and Chalcedon. The so-called neo-Chalcedonian theology resumed at the third Council of Constantinople (680-681) further made a notable contribution to an exact understanding of the close union of dogmatic and biblical theology. Only through this can we fully understand the sense of the Chalcedonian dogma (481).

In the manuals, the theological development after Chalcedon has ordinarily come to be little considered. The impression thus frequently remains that dogmatic Christology finishes up with a certain parallelism between the two natures of Christ. This impression has also been the cause leading to the divisions since Chalcedon. But in effect the declaration of the true humanity and the true divinity of Christ can retain its significance only when there is clarification also of the mode of unity of the two natures, which the Council of Chalcedon has defined by the formula of the 'one person' of Christ, at that time not yet fully examined. In fact only that unity of divinity and humanity which in Christ is not parallelism, where one stands alongside the other, but real compenetration — compenetration between

God and man — means salvation for humankind. Only thus in fact does that true 'being with God' take place, without which liberation and freedom do not exist.

This same query returned at the third Council of Constantinople (680-681) after two centuries of dramatic struggle, marked most often also by Byzantine politics. According to this Council, on the one hand: the unity between the divinity and the humanity in Christ does not in any sense imply an amputation or reduction of the humanity. If God joins himself to his creature — man/woman — he does not wound or diminish it: he brings it to its plenitude. But on the other hand (and this is no less important) there remains no trace of that dualism or parallelism of the two natures which in the course of history was frequently judged necessary to defend the human liberty of Jesus. Such studies forgot that the assumption of the human will into the divine will does not destroy freedom, but on the contrary generates true liberty. The Council of Constantinople has analysed concretely the problem of the two natures and one person in Christ in view of the problem of the will of Jesus. We are reminded firmly that there exists a specific will of the *man* Jesus that is not absorbed into the divine will. But this human will *follows* the divine will and thus becomes a single will with it, not, however, in a forced way but by way of freedom. The metaphysical duplicity of a human will and a divine will is not eliminated, but in the personal sphere, the area of freedom, there is accomplished a fusion of the two, so that this becomes not *one single natural will* but *one personal will.* This free union — a mode of union created by love — is a union higher and more intimate than a purely natural union. It corresponds to the highest union which can exist, the union of the Trinity. The Council explains this union by a saying of the Lord given in the Gospel of John: "I have come down from heaven, not to do my own will, but the will of the Father who sent me" (Jn 6,38). Here the *divine* Logos is speaking, and speaking of the *human* will of Jesus in the mode by which he calls *his* will the will of the Logos. With this exegesis of John 6,38, the Council proves the unity of the subject: in Jesus there are not two 'I', but only one. The Logos speaks of the will and human thought of Jesus using the 'I'; this has become his 'I', has been assumed into his 'I', because the human will has become fully one with the will of the Logos, and with it has become pure assent to the will of the Father.

Maximus the Confessor, the great theologian-exegete of this second phase of the development of Christological dogma, has illustrated those references to the prayer of Jesus in the Garden of Gethsemane, which we have already seen in the previous meditation, as the most clear expressions of the singular relationship of Jesus with God. In effect, in such prayer we can, so to speak, look into the inner life of the Word become man. We can see it in that phrase which remains the measure and model of all effective prayer: "Not what I will, but what thou wilt" (Mk 14,36). The human will of Jesus enters into the will of the Son. By doing so, it receives the identity of the Son, which consists in entire subordination of the I to the Thou, in the giving and transferring of the I to the Thou: this is the mode of being of the one who is pure relation and pure act. When the 'I' gives itself to the 'Thou', freedom originates, because the 'form of God' has been assumed.

But we can describe this process also and better still from another viewpoint: the Logos stoops to assume as his own the will of man, and speaks to the Father with the 'I' of this man, and thereby transforms the word of a man into the eternal word, into his own blessed "Yes, Father". While giving to this man his own 'I', his own identity, the Logos frees the man, saves him, divinises him. We here touch almost palpably on the reality meant by the phrase 'God became man': the Son transforms the anguish of a man into the obedience of the Son, transforms the speech of the 'servant' into the words of the 'Son'. Thus becomes comprehensible also our way of liberation, our sharing in the freedom of the Son.

In the unity of wills of which we have spoken is attained the greatest conceivable transformation of any person, which is at the same time the one thing ultimately desirable: divinisation. Thus the prayer which enters into the prayer of Jesus, and which in the body of Christ becomes the prayer of Jesus Christ, can be defined as the 'laboratory' of freedom. Here and in no other place occurs that profound change in a person which we need for the world to become better. Only on this road in fact does conscience attain its full rectitude and an irresistible strength. And only from this conscience can be born again that order in human affairs which corresponds to human dignity and which can defend it: an order which in every generation must be sought afresh by a vigilant human conscience, so that the Kingdom of God may come, a kingdom which God alone can build.

Chapter 4

The Paschal Mystery

1. Holy Thursday

The Hebrew Pasch was and is a family feast. It was not celebrated in the Temple, but at home. In the account of the Exodus the home already appears as the place of salvation and of refuge in that dark night of the passing over of the Angel of the Lord. In another way, that night in Egypt is an image of the power of death, of the destruction and chaos which are always rising up from the depths of the world and of human-kind, and which threaten to destroy the 'good' creation and transform the world into a desert, into something uninhabit-able. In this situation the home and the family offer a place of shelter; in other words, the world has to be continually defended from chaos, creation must always be protected and made new.

In the nomad calendar from which Israel took the paschal feast, the Pasch was the first day of the year; it was the day on which Israel had again to be defended against the threat of annihilation. The home and family are the protecting wall in life, the place in which we are safe and at peace, the peace of being together, which lets us live, and preserves creation.

In Jesus' time also, after the immolation of the lamb in the Temple, the Pasch was celebrated at home, in the family. It was prescribed that on the night of the Pasch no one could leave the city of Jerusalem. The whole city was considered the place of salvation against the night of chaos, and its walls as the barriers defending creation. Israel had to resort in pilgrimage to this city every year at the Pasch so as to go back to its begin-nings, be created anew, and receive anew its salvation libera-tion and foundation. In this there is great wisdom. In the course of a year a people is always in danger of dispersion not only exteriorly but also from within, and of losing the inner supports which govern it. It needs to return to its authentic foundations. The Pasch was to be this annual return of Israel, from the dangers of that disorder present in every people, to what had founded it and governed still, and been its steadfast defence, and to the recreation of its origins. And since Israel knew that over it shone the star of election, it knew besides that from its fortune or misfortune would be derived something for all the world, and that according to its existence or its fall the destiny of the world and of creation was at stake.

Jesus, too, celebrated the Pasch in compliance with the prescription: at home with his family, for the Apostles had become his new family. In this he was, on the other hand, obeying a precept then existing according to which the pilgrims who made their way to Jerusalem could form pilgrim groups called *chaburot* which for that night constituted a home and family for the Pasch. And so the Pasch has become a Christian feast also. We are the *chaburah* of Jesus, the family he has founded with his company of pilgrims, with the friends who travel the way of the Gospel with him through the land of history. As his pilgrim company we are his home; so the Church is the new family, the new city, and it is for us what Jerusalem was: that living home which keeps away the forces of evil and is the place of peace, which preserves creation, and us. The Church is the new city, Jesus' family, the living Jerusalem; her faith is a barrier and a wall against the threatening forces of chaos which seek to destroy the world. Her walls are fortified by the sign of the blood of Jesus Christ, that is by the love which goes on to the very end, and is without end. This love is the power able to fight against chaos, the creative power always founding anew the world, its peoples and its families; and in this way offering us *shalom*, the place of peace, in which we can live with one another, for one another, and protected by one another.

I believe there are many reasons why we should reflect further on such matters, related as they are to our day, and to let them speak to us. We see in fact the strength of chaos, we see how precisely in the midst of an advanced society, which seems to know and to be able to do everything, the primordial forces of chaos rise up against what society considers to be progress. We see how a people, in the very midst of their prosperity, their technical ability and their scientific mastery of the world, can be destroyed from within, and how creation can be threatened by the forces of chaos lurking in the depths of the human heart and threatening the world.

We know from experience that technology and money do not of themselves succeed in keeping at bay the capacity which chaos has for organisation. This can only be done by the real fortification which the Lord has given us and the new family he has formed for us. And I believe that for this reason the paschal feast, come down to us from the nomads by way of Israel and Christ, is, even in its deepest meaning, of eminent political importance. Here in Europe we also need to return as nations to our spiritual foundation, if we do not want to lose ourselves in self-destruction.

This feast should be once again today a feast of the family, the true bulwark for the defence of creation and humankind. Let us pray for this warning note to be heard once more for the family to be held in honour again from now on as a living home where humankind can grow, and chaos and emptiness are shut out. But we must add that the family, this setting for humankind, this protection for the creature, can continue to exist only whenever it is under the banner of the Lamb, when it is itself protected by the power of faith, and called into existence by the love of Jesus Christ. The family cannot survive by itself; it breaks up if it is not inserted in the larger family which gives it stability and security. Therefore this should be the night on which we pass along the way towards the new city, the new family, towards the Church, on which we enroll ourselves again, unshaken in our resolve, as in the new homeland of the heart.

There is another reflection to be made here. Israel inherited this festival from the worship and culture of the nomads. With them it was the Spring feast, the day of departure for a new migration with their flocks. A circle therefore was first of all traced round the tents with the blood of a lamb. This was intended almost as a defensive action against the forces of death, which were always to be met with in the unknown world of the desert. And the ceremony ended with the pilgrim feast, at the moment of departure, consisting of the food of the

nomad: lamb, bitter herbs instead of salt, and unleavened bread. During the time of their wanderings, Israel inherited these basic elements for their practice of the feast, and the Pasch always reminded them of the time when they were a homeless people, a wandering people without a country. This feast was always a reminder: even when we have a home, we are always nomads, as human beings we are never really at home, as human beings we are always on the way. And because we are journeying and because nothing belongs to us, everything that we have is in common, and we are for one another. The early Church translated this word *Pascha* by 'passage' and in this way expressed Christ's journey through death to the new life of the Resurrection. Therefore the Pasch has become and remained for us also a feast of pilgrimage; to us also it says: we are only guests on the earth, we are all God's guests. And so it encourages us to be brothers and sisters of our fellow guests, because we ourselves are only guests. We are only guests on the earth; our Lord, that is the One who himself becomes a guest and a nomad, calls us to be available to the suffering, the neglected, the imprisoned, the persecuted. He is in them all; and in the law of Israel, where norms are given for the time when the people settled down finally in the Promised Land, there are repeated perscriptions for wanderers to be treated as equals, and always with the reminder: "Remember that you were once a nomad and a wanderer!" We are nomads and pilgrims. That is how we ought to think of the earth and our life and our attitude to one another. We are only guests on the earth: but that makes us remember our own arcane pilgrimage, makes us remember that the earth is not our final goal, that we are journeying towards a new world and that the things of earth also are not last and final. We can scarcely dare to say so, because here we are reproached that Christians are not concerned with earthly things and have neglected to build the new city in this world because they thought they had a pretext for taking refuge in he next. But that is not true. People who throw themselves headlong into the world, for whom earth is the only heaven, such people make the earth a hell because they make of it what it cannot be: they want it to be final, and so they demand in this way something which sets it against itself, against truth, and against other people. No, when we know that we are nomads it is precisely then that we become free, free of the greed for possession; it is then that we become free for one another, and then that there is given us the responsibility of transforming the earth in such a way that one day we shall be able to lay it in the hands of God. Therefore this night is a passage which reminds us of Jesus' last journey, and of the need to bear in mind that one day we shall have to leave behind all that we possess, and that in the end it is not what we *have* that counts but only what we *are*; at the end we shall have to render an account of how in this world — on the basis of faith — we have been people who have mutually afforded each other peace, a homeland, a family, and the new city.

The Pasch was celebrated at home. Jesus did so too. But after the meal he got up and went out, went beyond the limits allowed by the Law by crossing the brook Kidron, the boundary of Jerusalem. He went out into the night. Not fearing chaos, not hiding from it, rather he went into its depths, even into the jaws of death: "He descended into hell", as we say in the Creed. He went out; and this means to say accordingly: though the ramparts of the Church are the faith and love of Jesus Christ, the Church is not a fortified citadel but an open city; and hence to believe means also to go out with Jesus Christ, not fearing chaos, because he is stronger, because he has gone there, and we, as we go out into it, are following him. To believe means to pass beyond the wall and into the midst of the chaotic world, to create with the strength of Jesus Christ a space for faith and love. The Lord went out: this is a sign of his strength. He went out into the night of Gethsemane, into the night of the Cross, the night of the tomb. He went out because his love bears within it the love of God, which has greater power than the forces of destruction. It is therefore precisely in this going forth, along the way of the Passion, that the victorious deed lies, and already in this mystery is to be found the mystery of paschal joy. He is the stronger, there is no power which could resist him and no place where he is not. He calls us to attempt the way with him because where there is faith and love, there he is, and there too is the strength of peace which overcomes death and emptiness.

At the end of the liturgy of Holy Thursday the Church

imitates Jesus' journey, carrying the Blessed Sacrament out of the tabernacle to a side chapel to represent the loneliness of Gethsemane, the loneliness of Jesus' mortal anguish. The faithful pray in the chapel, wanting to follow Jesus in the prayer of his loneliness so that it ceases to be loneliness. This way of Holy Thursday should not remain a mere gesture and liturgical sign, it should always be accounted for us as entering into his loneliness, seeking him always, despised, derided, there where he is alone, where people do not want to know him, and to be with him. This liturgical journey is for us an exhortation to seek the solitude of prayer. But also it invites us to seek him in those who are lonely, those nobody cares about, and to watch with him, and in the midst of the darkness to renew with him the light of life, which he is. It is his journey which has made the new day rise in this world, the life of the Resurrection which knows no night. In the Christian faith we obtain this promise.

Let us pray during this Lent that he may make his light shine on all the darkness of this world, and he may show us too, in the hour of loneliness and obscurity, that he is with us in the night and that he will raise up through us the new city of the world, the place of his peace and of the new creation.

2. The washing of the feet

In this meditation I should like to consider an aspect of the Johannine vision of the Paschal Mystery.

Many exegetes agree today in accepting that the Gospel of St John divides into two parts:

     a) a book of signs: chapters 2-12
     b) a book of glory: chapters 13-21

This arrangement already strongly accentuates the mystery of the triduum, the Paschal Mystery. The signs foretell and in advance interpret the reality of these days whose essential content is indicated by the word 'glory'.

1. Chapter 13 has a particular importance in this structure. Its first part expounds, by means of the symbolic gesture of the washing of the feet, the significance of the life and death of

Jesus. From this viewpoint the borderline between the life and death of Jesus fades; they appear as a single act in which Jesus, God's Son, washes the soiled feet of humankind. The Lord accepts and carries out the service of a slave, performing a humble task — the lowest task in the world — to make us fit for table, open to one another and to God, to accustom us to the worship, to the nearness, of God.

The action of the washing of the feet becomes for John the representation of what Jesus' whole life is: his rising from the table setting aside his garment of glory, bending down to us in the mystery of forgiveness, the service of his human life and death. The life and death of Jesus do not stand one alongside the other: the death of Jesus only goes to show the substance, the real content, of his life. Life and death become transparent and reveal the act of love to the last, an infinite love, which is the only true washing of humankind, the sole washing capable of enabling us for communion with God, capable, that is, of making us free. The content of the account of the washing of the feet can therefore be summed up as follows: taking our part, even if it means suffering, in the divine-human act of love, which is thereby the purification, that is the liberation, of humankind.

This Johannine vision contains various additional aspects also:

a) If it is so the unique condition of salvation is the 'yes' to the love of God rendered possible in Jesus. This affirmation does not express in any way an idea of general *apokatástasis*, which would mistakenly end by keeping God as a magician and would destroy human dignity and responsibility. Human beings have the power to refuse liberating love, and the Gospel shows two types of this refusal. The first is that of Judas. Judas represents the person who does not want to be loved, who thinks only of possessing, who lives solely for material things. For this reason St Paul says that avarice is idolatry (Col 3,5), and Jesus teaches us that we cannot serve two masters: the service of God and the service of Mammon exclude one another (Mt 6,24); the camel will not go through the needle's eye (Mk 10,25).

b) But there is also another type of refusal of God, not only that of materialism but also that of the devout person,

represented here by Peter. This is the danger called by St Pa
'judaism' and strongly criticised in the Pauline Letters: tl
danger that 'religious people' will not accept reality, nor tl
fact that they too have need of pardon, that their feet too a
dirty. The danger for pious people consists in thinking th
they have no need of God's goodness, and of not acceptir
grace: it is the danger of the elder son in the parable of tl
prodigal son, the danger of the workmen of the first hour (N
20,1-16), the danger of those who murmur and are enviou
because God is good.

In this perspective, to be Christian means allowing our fe
to be washed, or, in other words, believing.

2. We see then in the scene of the washing of the feet tha
the Evangelist interprets here not only Christology an
soteriology but also Christian anthropology. I should like t
note three points illustrating this statement:

a) Seen in this way, not only do the life and death of Jesu
cohere but also the sacraments of Baptism and Penance, whic
emerge from the font which is the love of Jesus: the life an
death of Jesus, and Baptism and Penance are together th
divine font opening the way to freedom and giving access t
the table of life.

b) This scene likewise interprets the spiritual content o
Baptism: the permanent 'yes' to love, with faith as the centra
act of the spiritual life.

c) Starting from these two points, an ecclesiology and
Christian ethic develop. To accept the washing of feet mean
entering into the Lord's action, sharing in it ourselves, lettin
ourselves be identified with that action. To receive this wash
ing means to continue with Christ to wash the soiled feet o
the world. Jesus says: "If I, then, your Lord and teacher, have
washed your feet, you also ought to wash one another's feet'
(13,14). These words are not a moral gloss on a dogmatic fact
but belong rather to the very centre of Christology. Love is
received only by loving. Fraternal love is, in John, inserted
into the trinitarian love. This is the 'new commandment', not
in the sense of an external command but as the inner structure
of the essence of Christianity. In this connection it can be
interesting to point out how St John never speaks of a love for

99

all people in general, but only of love within the fraternal community, that is, the baptised. Modern theologians criticise St John for this fact and speak of an unacceptable restriction of Christianity, of a loss of universality. Certainly, there is a danger here, and complementary texts, like the parable of the Good Samaritan and that of the Last Judgment, are indispensable. But taken in the context of the unity and indivisibility of the New Testament as a whole, John expresses a very important truth: love in the abstract will never have any force in the world if it does not sink its roots in the actual community built on fraternal love. Love's polity is constructed only by starting out from a small fraternal community. It has to begin from the particular to arrive at the universal. To make openings for fraternity is today no less important than in the time of St John, or of St Benedict, who with the fraternity of monks was the true architect of Christian Europe, building models of the new city in a fraternity of faith.

And now, returning to the Gospel, we can say that the account of the washing of the feet has a very literal content: the sacramental structure involves an ecclesial structure, a fraternal structure. This structure implies that Christians have to be ready to offer one another the service of slaves, and that only thus can they bring about the Christian revolution, and construct the New City.

3. I should like to add to this meditation the exegesis of St Augustine on the washing of the feet, in which the Bishop of Hippo interprets the tension in his life between contemplation and daily service.

a) In the first passage we shall consider, St Augustine reflects on the Lord's words: "He who has bathed does not need to wash, except for his feet, but he is clean all over" (Jn 13,10), and asks himself what is meant by that. One who has bathed, that is who has been baptised, is clean; why and in what sense is there need for washing his feet? What is this washing of feet always and repeatedly necessary after the bath, after Baptism that is? The Holy Doctor replies: Without doubt we are made clean interiorly in Baptism, feet as well; we have been made 'clean'; but while we have to go on living here below, our feet must walk on the soil of this world. "And thus

our human feelings themselves, which are inseparable from our human life on earth, are like feet wherewith we are brought into sensible contact with human affairs; and are so in such a way, that if we say we have no sin we deceive ourselves and the truth is not in us".[7] But the Lord stands before God and, interceding for us, washes our feet day after day, at the moment when we pronounce the prayer: Forgive us our trespasses. In the daily prayer of the Our Father, Jesus bends down to us, still today, takes a towel and washes our feet.

b) Following on this, St Augustine adds a reflection on another text of Scripture taken from the Song of Solomon, where he finds some verses at first puzzling to him, on this same subject, the washing of feet. In chapter 5 of the Song the following scene is found: The Bride is on her couch, asleep — her heart watches. At that moment she hears a shout; the Beloved is knocking: "Open to me, my sister". The Bride does not want to: 'I had put off my garment, how could I put it on? I had bathed my feet, how could I soil them?"

Here the reflection of the Holy Doctor begins. The Beloved knocking at the door of the Bride is Christ, the Lord. The Bride is the Church, the souls who love the Lord. But — says St Augustine — how can they soil their feet by going to the Lord, if they go to open the door to him? However could the way to Christ, who washes our feet, make those feet dirty? By such a paradox St Augustine reveals something crucial for his life as a pastor: his dilemma between his desire for prayer, silence, intimacy with God, and the necessity for administrative work, meetings pastoral life. The Bishop says: The Bride who does not want to open the door represents those contemplative people who seek complete retirement entire seclusion from the world, and want to live only in the beauty of truth and faith, leaving the world to itself. But Christ comes, shouts, awakes the soul, knocks on the door and says: "You are living in contemplation but you have shut the door on me. You seek leisure for just a few while outside there is a flood of evil and the love of the multitude grows cold. . .". The Lord knocks therefore to break into the repose of the holy idlers and calls: "Open to me . . . open to me and preach me to others". To say the truth, by opening the door, and going out on apostolic work, we inevitably soil our feet. But we soil them for Christ, while outside the crowd is waiting which we can join in no other way than by passing through the defilement of the world where they are.[8]

Thus St Augustine interprets his own destiny. After his conversion it had been his intention to found a monastery, leave the world for good, and live with friends for truth alone and contemplation. But in 391, with his unwilling ordination to the priesthood the Lord had ruined that repose, had knocked and gone on knocking day after day and calling out: "Open to me and preach me to others". Augustine had to learn to understand that this daily call was really the voice of Jesus, that Jesus was obliging him to go out into the uncleanness of the people (the holy Bishop was at this time also the *Khadi*, the civil judge) and that paradoxically it was precisely in this way that he was on the road towards Jesus, drawing near to the Lord. "Open to me and preach me to others". St Augustine's generous reply requires no comment: "But see, I rise and open — O Christ, wash our feet: forgive us our debts because our love is not altogether extinguished, for we also forgive our debtors. When we listen to thee the bones which have been humbled rejoice with thee in the heavenly places. But when we preach thee we have to tread the ground in order to open to thee; and then, if we are blameworthy we are troubled; if we are commended we become inflated. Wash our feet that were formerly cleansed, but have again been soiled in our walking through the earth to open unto thee".[9]

3. The connection between the Last Supper, the Cross and the Resurrection

In the meditation on the public life of Jesus we found that the prayer of Jesus is the key which opens up to us the intimate connection between Christology and soteriology; the key that reveals the person of Jesus and his work and suffering. Now let us apply this knowledge to the facts of the last days of Jesus' life. In thematic form we can say: Jesus died praying. At the Last Supper, at the moment in which he gave himself in the Eucharist, he accepted his death in anticipation and thus, from within, transformed his dying into an act of love, into a glorification of God.

Although the Evangelists' accounts of the last words of Jesus are divergent as to detail, they do however agree in the essential: according to all of them, Jesus died praying. He made of his death an act of prayer, an act of adoration. According to Matthew and Mark he cried "with a loud voice" the opening words of Psalm 21, the great Psalm of the just man suffering and set free: "My God, my God, why hast thou forsaken me?" (Mk 15,34; Mt 27,46).

Both these two Evangelists relate however that these words were not understood by the persons standing there who interpreted Jesus' cry as an appeal addressed to Elijah. According to them, then, faith alone has succeeded in understanding that this dying cry of Jesus was the messianic prayer of the great Psalm of Israel's suffering and hope, which concludes with the vision of the poor satisfied and all the ends of the earth returning to the Lord. This Psalm 21 was for primitive Christianity a key-text of Christology in which there found expression not only the death of Jesus on the Cross but equally the mystery of the Eucharist deriving from the Cross, the true satisfying of the 'poor' and the Church of the 'Gentiles' which derived in the same way from the Cross. So this cry in death, thought by those present to be a futile invocation of Elijah, became for Christians the most profound exposition which Jesus himself had given of his death. The theology of the Cross in this Psalm was so applied to him as though the prophecy contained in it was of himself. With the accomplishment of the prophecy, the truth of this application became apparent, and the Psalm proved to be the very words of Jesus, this prayer being in truth meant for none other than himself, abandoned, despised but accepted and glorified by the Father. It should be added that the whole story of the passion is shot through with the threads of this Psalm, weaving in and out continually in an interchange between words and realiy. The archetypal suffering which this Psalm indicates without naming it has here become real and actual; here is accomplished that suffering originally of a just man apparently repudiated by God. It thus becomes clear that Jesus is the true subject of this Psalm, that he bore that suffering from which springs the food of the poor ones and the conversion of the nations to the glory of the God of Israel.

But let us return to our starting point. As we have seen, there is not one simple account of what precisely were the last words of Jesus. Luke has not taken them specifically from Psalm 21 but from that other great Psalm of the passion, the 31st, at verse 6 (Lk 23,46); John has chosen another verse of Psalm 21, verse 15, and set it with the Psalm of the passion, the 68th (Jn 19,28ff). The accounts of all the Evangelists are unanimous on three points, on which therefore any theological interpretation should be centred.

1. Common to all the Evangelists is the conviction that Psalm 21 is in a particular manner in line with the passion of Jesus, as much by its objective reality as by the personal acceptance of the passion on the part of Jesus; and moreover it is certain that they always consider the Psalm to be an indivisible whole.

2. All, furthermore, agree that Jesus' last words constituted the expression of his obedience without reserve to the will of the Father; the last word of Jesus was, according to them, not an invocation directed to some other man but to him, to be in dialogue with whom was Jesus' ultimate essence. All the Evangelists, therefore, are in agreement that the very dying of Jesus was an act of prayer, that such a death was a passing to the Father. All are in agreement that he prayed with the Scriptures and that in him Scripture became flesh, a true passion, passion of the Just One. All are consequently unanimous in maintaining that his death was made one with the word of God as his life had been, and that the word lived in him and was manifested in him.

When these things are considered there can equally be seen the inseparable connection between the Last Supper and Jesus' death. The words pronounced at the point of death and the words at the Last Supper, the reality of the death and the reality of the Last Supper, are set one against the other. The momentous event of the Last Supper consists in the fact that Jesus distributes his Body and his Blood, his earthly existence, in giving himself. To put this in other words: what took place at the Last Supper is an anticipation of the death, the transformation of the death into an act of love. Only in this context can we understand what it is that John means when he calls the death of Jesus a glorification of God and a glorification of the Son (Jn 12,28; 17,21). Death which by its nature is the end, the destruction of every relationship, is by him transformed into an act of communication of himself; and this is the salvation of humankind, in that it signifies that love conquers death. We can also express the same thing from another angle: death, which is the end of word and the end of life, itself becomes word and life, giving itself in oblation.

The death of Jesus thus affords us the key to understanding the Last Supper, and the Supper is the anticipation of the death, the transformation of a violent death into a voluntary sacrifice, in that act of love which is the redemption of the world.

The death without the Supper would be empty, without meaning; the Supper without the actual realisation of the death it anticipated would be a gesture without reality. Supper and Cross together are the only and inseparable source of the Eucharist. The Eucharist does not spring from the Supper alone; it springs from this oneness of Supper and Cross, as St John shows in his great image of the oneness of Jesus, Church and sacraments: that from the pierced side of the Lord "there came out blood and water" (19,34): Baptism and Eucharist, the Church, the new Eve.

Therefore the Eucharist is not simply Supper, and the Catholic Church intentionally did not call it 'Supper' to avoid this wrong impression. The Eucharist is the presence of Christ's Sacrifice, that supreme act of adoration which is at the same time an act of supreme love, love "to the end" (Jn 13,1), and thus it is Christ distributing himself under the figure of bread and wine.

If we now consider briefly the words of the institution of the Eucharist, we can see still more closely the union between Supper and Cross. Let us begin with the central words: "This is my body, this is my blood". The words used here stem from the sacrificial terminology of the Old Testament; according to this terminology they signify the sacrificial gifts in the Temple. By adopting this phraseology, and transforming it by making it personal, Jesus expresses that he is the real and definitive sacrifice, desired and willed in all the sacrifices of the Old Testament. The animals, beginning with the ram caught by the horns in a thicket and substituted for Isaac, were the substitutes for the true sacrifice. By his words here Jesus shows that Moses wrote of him (Jn 5,46). All the sacrifices are leaps towards him: God has no need of bulls and calves; God looks for that infinite love which alone is the true reconciliation between heaven and earth.

To these words stemming from the theology of the worship of Israel and the theology of the covenant established on Sinai, Jesus adds a phrase of prophetic origin: "given for you", "poured out for many for the remission of sins". These words are found in the Songs of the Servant of God handed down to us in the book of the prophet Isaiah. These Songs presuppose the exilic period: Israel no longer has its Temple, the only legitimate place in which to adore God. So it seems exiled from God also — forlorn in the desert. No longer can sacrifices of expiation and praise be offered. The inevitable question arises: how can there now exist any relationship with God, on which depends the salvation of the people and of the world? In this passion, in this suffering of a life lived away from their homeland, a life far from their own culture, Israel underwent a new experience: the solemn praises of God could no longer be celebrated. The only possibility for drawing near to God was suffering for God. Inspired by the Holy Spirit, the Prophets understood that the suffering of believing Israel was the true sacrifice, the new liturgy, and that in this true liturgy Israel represented the world before the face of God. This thinking was at the same time a consolation, an imperative and a hope. A consolation: Israel knew that in their passion especially they were drawing near to God, that in this, God was making them the light of the Gentiles. An imperative: they were conscious of having to accept their passion from the hands of God and to transform it through faith into an act of praise of God, into a liturgy of life. A hope: Israel realised that this figure of the Servant of God was greater than any individual, greater than the Prophets, than their whole nation. Israel understood that this figure was a 'sacramentum futuri', a sacrament of things to come. The hope found in their passion was that the suffering people were an anticipation of the true servant of God, and so, as 'sacramentum futuri', shared in his grace. By applying to the Last Supper these words about the Servant of God, Jesus says: I am this Servant of God. My passion and death are that definitive liturgy, that glorification of God which is the light and salvation of the world.

Here we touch upon an important point for the celebration of the Eucharist. Israel concelebrated the Eucharist with Jesus, in that they shared in the sufferings of the Servant of God. To participate in the Eucharist, to communicate with the body and blood of Christ, demands the liturgy of our life, a sharing in the passion of the Servant of God. In this participation our sufferings become 'sacrifice' and so we can complete "in [our] flesh what is lacking in Christ's afflictions" (Col 1,24).

It seems to me that this aspect of Eucharistic devotion has been somewhat obscured in the liturgical movement and that we ought to recover it. In the communion of suffering, sacramental communion is actualised, we enter into the riches of the Lord's mercy, and from this com-passion springs up anew the capacity to be merciful — from which come the vocations which make mercy their aim and which are lacking today in the Church.

Let us return to the words of Jesus at the Last Supper. We have found the Mosaic tradition and the Isaian prophetic tradition in these words. There is still a third current to be found here, the theology of Jeremiah, very close to the Wisdom theology of the last century of the Old Testament. Jesus says: "This cup is the *new* covenant in my blood" (Lk 22,20), and thus gives the promise of a new covenant rooted in the prophecy of Jeremiah (Jer 31,31). Jeremiah foresees a new covenant, centred not on Sinai but on Sion; its law is to be inscribed on the tablets of the heart and founded on forgiveness of sins. Jesus says that at the moment of his death this new covenant will come about; with his blood the new law will be inscribed in our hearts: "A new commandment I give to you, that you love one another; even as I have loved you, that you also love one another" (Jn 13,34). With each sacramental communion Jesus writes afresh the new law on our hearts. St Thomas interprets this fact exacly when he says that 'caritas' is the 'res sacramenti' of the Eucharist (Love is what constitutes the sacrament).

One final observation. If we have at length interpreted the

connection between Supper and Cross, we have in fact all the time been speaking also of the Resurrection. Not only are Supper and Cross inseparable: Supper, Cross and Resurrection form the one indivisible Paschal Mystery. The theology of the Cross is the Resurrection, therefore the Resurrection is the divine response and the divine interpretation of the Cross. The theology of the Cross is a paschal theology, a theology of joyous victory even in this valley of tears. We have shown that the Last Supper was the anticipation of the violent death of Jesus, and that the Cross without the Supper, the Supper without the reality of the Cross, would remain void. Now we have to add that the Last Supper also anticipates the Resurrection, the certainty that love is stronger than death. This act of love to the last is the transubstantiation of the death, its radical transformation, the power of the Resurrection already present in the shadow of death. The Supper without the Cross, the Cross without the Supper, would be void, but the two without the Resurrection would be the wreck of hope. The image of the pierced side, fount of water and blood, is also the image of the Resurrection, of the love stronger than death. In the Eucharist we receive this love — we receive the medicine of immortality. The Eucharist guides us to the fount of true life, of invincible life, and shows us where and how true life is to be found — not in riches and possessions, not in having. Only if we follow Jesus on the way of his Cross, do we find ourselves on the road to life.

To this biblical meditation let us also add an anthropological consideration. To be human beings means going towards death. To be human means having to die, being in that substance of contradiction where, in the biological perspective, it is natural and necessary to die; but at the same time there is in physical life a spiritual centre which aspires to eternity, and from this point of view to die is not natural but illogical, because it means expulsion from the sphere of loving, destruction of that connecting element which is the desire of eternity.

To live means, in this world, to die. That the Son of God 'was made man' means therefore this also: he walked towards death. The contradiction inherent in human death reaches its culmination in Jesus. In him in fact, he who remained fully in communion with the Father, death in its absolute solitariness is entirely incomprehensible. On the other hand death holds for him a specific necessity. We have in fact already seen that precisely his being with the Father is the reason for the incomprehension of the people in respect of him, and therefore for his solitude in the midst of his public life. His capital punishment is the final act consequent on this incomprehension, the relegation of what is misunderstood to a zone of silence.

From this can perhaps be seen something of the interior theological dimension of his death, because to die is always for a human being a biological happening and at the same time spiritual and human. The destruction of the body, the instrument of communication, here interrupts the dialogue with the Father. When the human instrument comes to fall away, the spiritual action which is founded on it also disappears, temporarily. Thus something more is shattered here than in any ordinary death. There is an interruption of that dialogue which in reality is the axis of the whole world. The cry of agony in Psalm 21, "My God, my God, why hast thou forsaken me", makes us perceive something of the depths of this process. But just as Jesus had isolated this dialogue and had motived the particular character of his death, so, in this dialogue, the Resurrection is already present, even in the shadow of death. Because the dialogue with the Father is also the fixed centre in the human being of Jesus, his humanity is hidden in that very Trinitarian exchange of eternal love. Thus, likewise, this humanity can no longer fade, it is fixed on the rock of eternal love; as a result, it necessarily rises again from death and resumes once more its human fulness — the indivisible unity of soul and body.

The Resurrection reveals what is the decisive article of our faith: "He was made man". From this we know what is forever true: he *is* man. This he remains for ever. Humanity through him has been made to enter into the very nature of God: this is the fruit of his death. We are *in* God. God is the entirely other, and at the same time the not-other. If together with Jesus we say Father, we say it in God himself. This is the hope of humankind, the Christian joy, the Gospel: he is man, still today. In him God is truly become not-other. Humankind, the absurd, is no longer absurd. The human race, disconsolate, is no longer disconsolate: we should rejoice. He loves us; and God loves us to such a point that his love has been made flesh and remains flesh. This joy should be the strongest impulse of all, that most explosive force which impels us to communicate the news to all people, so that they likewise may rejoice in the light which is revealed to us, and which in the midst of the world's night announces the day.

4. Risen on the third day

The controversy on the Resurrection of Jesus from the dead has broken out again with renewed intensity and this time within the Church. It is fed not only by the general crisis in inherited values but especially by the form of tradition in which it comes to our notice. The fact that the biblical texts have to be translated not only linguistically but also conceptually from the world as it then was to that of today, makes it likely that even at this point it may be necessary to have a process of translation that makes most of the usual objections fall. This impression comes to be still further reinforced if the various Resurrection accounts are compared. Their differences then appear evident and it becomes clear that they are making an effort even though in stammering fashion to turn into words an event for which ordinary language does not seem to offer sufficient possibilities of expression. The problem of knowing which things are central and which are peripheral becomes all the more pressing, the more it becomes difficult to decide between counterfeit and true tradition.

I shall not set out in this meditation to discuss the individual theories which exist today on the subject, but as far as possible I shall seek to bring out in positive fashion the heart of the biblical testimony. It does not take much effort to discover, on reading the New Testament, that there exist two noticeably different types of tradition concerning the Resurrection: the one I shall call the confessional tradition, and the other I shall call the narrative tradition. As an example of the first type we find verses 3-8 of chapter 15 of the First Letter to the Corinthians; we meet the second type in the account of the Resurrection by the four Evangelists. Both types have different origins, pose very different problems, and have a dissimilar intent and purpose. In consequence, likewise, what they call for is different, and this is of notable importance for their interpretation, for the kernel of their message.

We can perceive the origin of the confessional tradition in the narrative tradition. This tells how the disciples from Emmaus were greeted by the Eleven at their return home with the announcement: "The Lord is truly risen and has appeared to Peter" (Lk 24,34). This passage is perhaps the oldest text we possess on the Resurrection. Whether it is so or not, the formation of the tradition begins with simple proclamations such as this, which little by little became a fundamental element of it, solidly formulated in the assembly of the disciples. They developed formulas of the profession of faith in the presence of the Lord which are precisely the fundamental expression of the Christian hope, and which had moreover the function of being a sign of the believers among themselves.

The Christian confession was born. In this process of tradition very quickly grew up, in and around the confines of Palestine and probably in the years 30-40 A.D., that confession which Paul has preserved for us in his first Letter to the Corinthians (15,3-8), as being a tradition which he himself received from the Church and which he faithfully transmits. In these confessional texts, and they are the most ancient, the handing on of individual attestations is only a very secondary consideration; the real intention, as Paul emphatically underlines, is to maintain the Christian nucleus, without which both message and faith would be vain.

Narrative tradition is stimulated into growth by something different. People want to know how things were. The desire for nearness, for details, was increasing. Along with this went, very soon, a necessity for Christian self-defence: against suspects and against attacks of all kinds which we can guess from the Gospel, and also against differing interpretations, such as were already creeping in at Corinth. All this acts as a stimulus to seeking out more satisfying pieces of information. It was on the basis of requirements such as these that a deeper tradition of the Gospels was formed. Both of these traditions have therefore their rightful importance; but at the same time it became evident that a hierarchy exists: the confessional tradition is above the narrative tradition. It is the *fides quae* (what must be

111

believed) the measure by which any interpretation is to be gauged.

Let us try then to understand more exactly that fundamental Credo which Paul has preserved; any attempt to arrive at decisions in the polemic between opinions must begin from here. Paul, or rather his Credo, begins with the death of Jesus. It is surprising that this text, which is so bare, not containing a word too many, makes two additions to the announcement "he died". One of these additions is this: "according to the scriptures", the other: "for our sins". What do they signify? The expression 'according to the Scriptures' sets the event in relation to the history of the Old Testament covenant of God with his people: this death is not incongruous, but forms part of the fabric of God's history, draws its logic from it and its significance. It is an event in which words of the Scriptures are fulfilled, or, rather, an occurrence which bears within it a logos, a logic: it comes from the word and penetrates into the word, spanning and fulfilling it. This death results from the fact that the word of God has been brought to humankind. How this insertion of death into the word of God should be interpreted is indicated by the second addition: he died "for sins". With this formula our Credo resumes a prophetic passage (Is 53,12; cf. also 53,7-11). Its reference to Scripture is not in the vague; it echoes a theme of the Old Testament which was well known in the time of the earliest assembly of witnesses. Thus in actual fact the death of Jesus comes to be withdrawn from that line of death, heavy with malediction, which derived from the dawn of consciousness of good and evil, from the presumption of equality with God which ends with the divine judgment: You shall return to the earth because from it you were taken. This death is of another kind. It is not an accomplishment of justice, which throws back humankind to the earth, but is the accomplishment of a love which will not let the other go without a word, without meaning, without eternity. It is not rooted in the sentence of expulsion from paradise but in the Songs of the Servant of God; it is a death which springs not from that sentence but from these Songs, and so a death which becomes a light for the peoples, a death in relation to the service of expiation, which seeks to bring reconciliation; a death, then, to put an end to death. Examined more closely the double interpretation which our Credo adds to the brief expression "he died", opens the way from the Cross to the Resurrection; what is said here ("died for our sins according to the Scriptures") is more than an interpretation: it forms part of the very event.

Now there follows in the text from Scripture, without comment, the phrase "was buried". But this can be understood only if it is seen in the context of what precedes and what follows. It affirms first of all that Jesus really experienced death in its totality. That he was laid in the grave of death. That he descended to the world of the dead, to hell. The faith of the Church has repeatedly studied in depth this mystery of the death of Jesus and sought to understand here the historical and universal extent of Jesus' victory. Today we are stimulated by another question: has the tomb a meaning for faith? Has it a relationship with the Lord's Resurrection? On this very point there are to be observed today a number of contrasting opinions, the controversy, that is, on the type of realism the Christian message really calls for. There are on the subject very attractive considerations. Bultmann, for example, asks himself what is signified by the miracle of a re-animated corpse. What use is it? Is it fitting for the word of God to be conflicting with the natural law? Is there not some doubt that it could concern us now in our day? But others wonder conversely: to transform the Resurrection event into a recognition of a call, of a continuing mission, of a lasting significance of Jesus, is not this perhaps after all an expedient that removes from the Resurrection its character of reality? To refute contemptuously what has come to be called the miracle of the re-animated corpse, would not this in reality be to conceal a contempt for the body which is as non-Christian as humanly wrong? Is there not hidden here perhaps a secret scepticism which would remove the possibility of God's action in the world? What promise can there be for us when no promise comes for the human body?

It must certainly be admitted that our Credo does not speak of an empty tomb. It is not directly interested in the fact of the tomb being empty, but that Jesus should have lain there. There is a need also to admit that to develop an understanding of the Resurrection starting from the empty tomb, as against the burial, does not tie in with the sense of the New Testament message.

In fact Jesus is not one who has 'returned' from the dead, like for example the young man of Naim and Lazarus, called back again to an earthly life, which then had to end in a final death. The Resurrection of Jesus is not, for example, an overcoming of clinical death, which we also know about today, which must however at a certain moment end in a clinical death without return. That matters do not stand like this is not only shown by the Evangelists, but also by the same Credo of Paul's (1 Cor 15,3-11) in so far as it describes the successive appearances of the risen Jesus with the Greek word *óphthe*, customarily translated as 'he appeared'; perhaps we should say more correctly; 'made himself seen'. This formula would make clear that what is treated of here is something different: that Jesus, after the Resurrection, belongs to a sphere of reality which is normally withdrawn from our senses. Only so can it be explained that Jesus was not recognised, as all the Evangelists agree in telling us. He no longer belongs to the world perceptible to the senses, but to the world of God. He can therefore be seen only by one to whom he grants it. And involved also in such a way of seeing are likewise the heart, the spirit, the whole inward person. Even in everyday life, seeing is not that simple process we generally take it to be. Two people looking at the world at the same time rarely see the same thing. Moreover seeing is always from within. According to circumstances, one person can perceive the *beauty* of things or only their *usefulness*; one can read in another's countenance preoccupation, love, hidden suffering, dissimulation, or notice nothing. All of this appears manifest to the sense also but comes however to be perceived only by a process of the mind and senses together, which is all the more demanding, the more profoundly the sensible manifestation of a thing arises from the depths of reality. Something analogous is true of the risen Lord: he manifested himself to the *senses*, and yet can stimulate only those senses that see better than through the senses.

Taking the whole passage into account, we should then admit that Jesus did not live like a re-animated corpse but in virtue of divine power, beyond the region of what is physically and chemically measurable. But it is also true that he himself, this person, the Jesus sentenced two days earlier, was alive. Our text (1 Cor 15,3-11) says so most explicitly, when it makes two separate statements one after the other. First is said that "he was raised on the third day in accordance with the Scriptures", and straight after that "he appeared to Peter, then to the twelve". Resurrection and appearance are two distinct facts, clearly separated in the confession. The Resurrection does not come to an end with the appearances. The appearances are not the Resurrection, but only its reflection. Before all this it is an *event* for Jesus *himself*, occurring between him and the Father in virtue of the power of the Holy Spirit; then the event happening to Jesus himself becomes *accessible* to other *people* because it is he who makes it accessible. And with this we are back again at the question of the tomb, for which the answer is now found. The tomb is not the central point of the message of the Resurrection; it is instead the Lord in his new life. But the tomb is nevertheless not to be taken away from the message. If the burial comes to be mentioned only in terse fashion in this extremely dense text, it is very clearly to be understood thereby that this was not the final state of Jesus' earthly life. Already the formulation which follows, the proclamation of the Resurrection "on the third day in accordance with the Scriptures", is a hidden allusion to Psalm 16,10. This text is one of the principal elements of the Old Testament evolved in primitive Christianity to demonstrate the messianic character of Jesus. According to the testimony of the preaching handed down in the Acts of the Apostles, the Psalm was the chief reference in the formula: "in accordance with the Scriptures". That verse, according to the Septuagint, which was the Old Testament for the early Church, says thus: "You will not abandon my life to the grave, nor let your holy one see corruption". According to the Jewish interpretation, corruption began after the third day; the word of Scripture is fulfilled in Jesus because he rises on the third day, before corruption begins. Here the text is also linked to the verse concerning his death: all this comes in the context of the Scriptures — the death of Jesus reached as far as the tomb but not as far as decomposition. He is the death of death, death hidden in the word of God and therefore related to life: which takes death's power away when, by the destruction of the body, human beings are destroyed by it in the earth.

Such a victory over the power of death, precisely where death displays its irrevocable nature, belongs centrally to the biblical testimony, quite apart from the fact that it would have been absolutely impossible to announce the Resurrection of Jesus from the moment that anyone could know and confirm that he was lying in the sepulchre. The thing would be impossible in our society, which experiments theoretically with resurrection concepts, for which the presence of the body is a matter of indifference; and it was certainly impossible in the Jewish world, for which a person was identified with the body and not with something apart from it. Anyone professing resurrection of the body is not affirming an absurd miracle but affirming the power of God, who *respects* his creation, without being tied to the law of its death. Indubitably death is the typical form of things in the world as it actually exists. But the overcoming of death, its real, not simply its conceptual elimination, is still today, as it was then, the object and desire of human research. The Resurrection of Jesus says that this victory is in effect possible, that death does not belong principally and irrevocably to the structure of the creature, to matter. Certainly it also says that to overcome the confines of death is not possible, definitively, by sophisticated clinical methods, through technology. This comes about through the creative power of the word and of love. Only these powers are sufficiently strong to modify so fundamentally the structure of matter, to make it possible to overcome the barrier of death. Hence in the extraordinary promise of this event there is also found an extraordinary call, a vocation, a whole interpretation of human existence and the existence of the world. But especially, it becomes manifest in this way that faith in the Resurrection of Jesus is a profession of the real existence of God and a profession of his creation, of the unconditional 'Yes' with which God stands before creation, before matter. The word of God truly penetrates to the heart of the body. His power does not end at the confines of matter. It embraces everything. And therefore also responsibility before this word certainly permeates matter and the body, and is there affirmed. Quite definitely, this is what faith in the Resurrection is concerned with: the real power of God, and the purport of human responsibility. That the power of God is hope and joy: this is the liberation revealed at Easter. In the Pasch, God reveals himself, his power — superior to the power of death — the power of the love of the Trinity. So the paschal revelation gives us the right to sing 'Alleluia' in a world overcast with the cloud of death.

NOTES

1. J. Jeremias, *Neutestametliche Theologie*, I, Gütersloh 1971.
2. S. Harkianakis, *Orthodoxe Kirche und Katholizismus*, München 1975; cf. Plato, *Timaios* 22b.
3. H. U. von Balthasar, *Hans des Gebetes*, in W. Sedel, *Kirche aus lebendigen Steinen*, Mainz 1975.
4. Harkianakis, *op. cit.*
5. Th. Maertens & J. Frisque, *Kommentar zum Messbuch*, I, Freiburg 1965.
6. M. Carrouges, *Charles de Foucauld*, Freiburg 1958.
7. St Augustine, *Treatise on John*, LVI, 4 C Chr XXXVI, 468.
8. *Ibid.*, LVII, 2-6; cf. J. Ratzinger, *Die Kirche in der Froömmigkeit des heilegen Augustinus*, in J. Daniélou & H. Vogrimler, *Sentire Ecclesiam*, Freiburg 1961.
9. *Ibid.*, LVII, 6.

Part III

Christ, the Church, the Priesthood

Chapter 1

Christ and his Church

1. Unity of Christology and Ecclesiology

In modern theology a rift has developed between Jesus and
the Church, a gap not only in theory, but translated into an
attitude expressed by the well-known slogan: 'Jesus yes,
Church no'. In this conference I should like to show how
ecclesiology springs necessarily from a Christological centre,
how the Church is preformed in the mystery of Jesus, so that
the two form fundamentally a single mystery.

Let us ask ourselves first: how can we know Jesus? How can
we approach him? The modern reply, today generally accepted
as obvious, is very simple: we know Jesus in the same way as
any other reality, that is through science. I would say: certainly, we know some other things about him by scientific
method. But there remains the question whether it is possible
by science alone to arrive at the presence of Jesus, Jesus in the
present, or whether — on the contrary — science ends logically
by emphasising his absence, the irrevocable absence of the
historical past. Or in other words: do we come near him in this
way, or do we collide at an infinite distance? There is an
important and incontestable answer to this, formulated ninety
years ago by Albert Schweitzer, summing up the effects of
scientific research on the story of Jesus: "This research —
Schweitzer says — had strange results. It began by rediscover-
ing the historical Jesus, thinking it was possible to transfer him,
as he was, into our time, as teacher and saviour. This freed
him from the chain which bound him for centuries to the rock
of Church doctrine. It was a rejoicing to see life and movement
return to this figure which seemed to be moving towards us.

121

But this Jesus did not stay: he went on past our time and back to his own".

Science of itself alone is not capable of recreating the past in the present and least of all for a personal relationship, but confirms and establishes the distance, the absence. Thus we can formulate — continuing the considerations of Part II — the following thesis: Given that prayer is central to the person of Jesus, sharing in his prayer is the prerequisite for knowing and understanding Jesus.

We begin here with a very ordinary consideration. Knowing depends by its nature on a certain conformity between the knower and the known. On this the ancient axiom holds that like knows like. In reference to spiritual dispositions and to persons, this means that to know requires a certain relationship of sympathy (*sym-pathein*), by means of which a person enters, so to say, into the person in question, into the corresponding spiritual reality, becomes one with it and in consequence is capable of understanding it (intellegere, to understand = intus legere, to read in). Let us develop this fact further with an example or two. One can only practise philosophy by philosophising, or following philosophical thought; mathematics is only grasped by thinking mathematically; medicine can only be acquired by exercising the art of medicine and not through books or reflection alone. In the same way also religion can be understood only through religion: this is an indisputable axiom of the philosophy of religion.

The fundamental act of religion is prayer, which in the Christian religion maintains an entirely specific characteristic of its own: it is transferring oneself into the body of Christ; an act of love then which, as love for and with the body of Christ, and also as love of neighbour, as love of the members of that body, necessarily and always recognises and complements our love of God.

In the preceding meditations we have seen that prayer was the act central to the person of Jesus, that his person comes to be identified by the act of prayer, by his constant communication with him whom he calls 'Father'. If this is true, a real understanding of his person is possible only if one enters into this act of prayer, if one shares in it. An indication of this

fact is found in the words of Jesus: "no one can come to me unless the Father who sent me draws him" (Jn 6,44). Where the Father is not, neither is there the Son. Where there is no relationship with God, there also remains incomprehensible a man whose very existence is relationship with God, with the Father; although, without doubt, we can come to know various aspects of him. Sharing then in the intimacy of Jesus, or in his prayer, which as we have seen means an act of love, giving oneself and handing oneself over to others, cannot be cast aside as some act or other of devotion which would not contribute anything much to true knowledge of him and which could in the end obstruct the rigid purity of critical science. Entirely to the contrary, such participation is instead the fundamental presupposition by which we can attain to a real understanding of him, in the sense of contemporary hermeneutics, that is entering into his time and into his spirit, absorbing them into oneself.

This is the state of the matter at all times apparent in the New Testament, which thus prepares the fundamental elements for a doctrine of theological knowledge. I will give only one example. When Ananias was sent to Paul to bring him into the Church, since he had a certain hesitation and suspicion about that man it was said to him as motivation: Go to him; "for behold, he is praying" (Acts 9,11). In prayer Paul arrived at that moment when he began to be one who sees, freed from blindness, not only exterior but also interior blindness. Anyone who prays begins to see; to pray and to see interact because, as says Richard of St Victor, "love is an eye". Therefore effective advances in Christology cannot ever derive from purely academic theology, not even from the modern theology which, in critical exegesis, in the history of dogma, in anthropology, pursues human sciences and other disciplines. All this is important, important as academic studies are. But it is not enough: we also need the theology of the Saints, the theology which derives from a concrete experience of divine reality. All the effective advances in theological knowledge have their origin in the eye of love, in the strength of its gaze. But having arrived at this point we have still to complete our thesis and say: communion with the prayer of Jesus includes communion with all his brethren. Coexistence with his person, which derives from participation in his prayer, constitutes that wider coexistence which Paul terms 'the body of Christ'. Therefore the Church, the 'body of Christ', is the true subject of knowledge of Jesus. In her memory the past is present, because Christ is in her and lives in the present.

When Jesus taught his disciples to pray, he told them to say: 'Our Father" (Mt 6,9). No one except he could say 'My Father'. All others have the right to pray to God as Father only in the community of that 'we' which Jesus inaugurated, because they are all created by God and created for one another. To assume and recognise the fatherhood of God always means: 'being turned towards one another'. We can of right call God "Father", in the measure with which we are inserted in that 'we' in which God's love searches for us. This correlation is based on a perspective of human reason and historical experience. We cannot any of us by our own powers construct a bridge to the infinite. No human voice is strong enough of itself to call to the infinite. There is no mind so acute as to be capable of conceiving with certainty what God is, whether he is listening, how to behave fittingly before him. Therefore throughout the history of the religions and of philosophy we can point to a certain dissension on the problem of God. On the one hand there has always existed firm basic evidence of the reality of God, and this fundamental evidence exists still today. The reality which Paul observes in the Letter to the Romans, with reference to the Book of Wisdom in the Old Testament (Wis 13,4ff), that is, that the Creator is visible in his creation and therefore can be known (Rom 1,19ff), is not at all a dogmatic postulate but an objective statement which is confirmed by the history of religions. But Paul, taking up again and deepening the thought of the Book of Wisdom, adds that this evidence is accompanied at the same pace by an enormous darkening and overturning of the image of God. This, too, is simply a description of fact, because the existence of God was and always is accompanied by immense mystery.

Scarcely does an attempt come to be made to describe this God more closely and give him a name, to bring humankind into relationship with him and to respond to him, than the image of God breaks up into contradictory representations which not only eliminate the primary evidence, but can obscure it to the point of unrecognisability, and in the extreme case can destroy it completely.

Something similar again emerges from observation of the history of religions. The theme of Revelation regularly recurs. Accordingly there can observed first of all, negatively, the idea that the human being is not by itself in a position to establish relations with the divine. Human beings know they cannot oblige the divinity to enter into relations with them. This means, positively, that the possible modes of relationship with God are reverted to the initiative of the divinity, who has been proclaimed by the wisdom of the ancients within the framework of a community which has handed it on as a tradition. Seen in this way, the realisation that religion must be founded on an authority higher than one's own reason and that it needs the community to sustain it, belongs to the fundamental consciousness of humankind, however diverse the variations, distortions even included.

At this point we should turn again to the figure of Jesus. However much Jesus found himself in an entirely special relationship with God, he clearly did not abandon the basic model just now described of the necessity of a community founded on the authority of Revelation which is handed down within that community as the place and condition for religious life. He lived his religious life in the framework of the faith and the tradition of God's people, Israel. His unceasing dialogue with the God of the Patriarchs, his Father, was also a communion with Moses and Elijah (cf. Mk 9,4). In this dialogue he went beyond the *letter* of the Old Testament and bared the *spirit*, to reveal the Father 'in the Spirit'. This victory over the letter of the Old Testament did not destroy the letter, that is the common religious tradition of Israel, but brought it to its fulness, 'fulfilled' it. Therefore neither did this dialogue constitute a diminution of the reality of 'God's people', but its true renewal. Breaking down the wall of the 'letter' opened to the people the entrance into the spirit of the tradition and thus access to the God of the Patriarchs, the God of Jesus Christ. For tradition to become universal is its highest confirmation, not the end of it nor its replacement by another. This should be understood here, for in fact it becomes clear that Jesus had no need to found a people of God (the 'Church'). It was

125

there already. What Jesus had to do was only to renew that people by deepening their relationship with God and to make it accessible to the whole of humankind.

In consequence the question whether Jesus had wanted to found a Church is not the right question, because it does not correspond to the real historical problem. The exact grounding of the question can only be whether Jesus had wanted to abolish the people of God already existing, or to renew it. The reply to this precise query is clear. Jesus renewed the ancient people of God, making it become a new people by inserting all those who believe in him into his own community (his 'body'). He did this in the moment when he transformed his death into an act of prayer, an act of love, thus making himself communicable. It could also consequently be said that Jesus, his message and his whole person, became part of Israel — God's people — subject to the already existing tradition, and thereby rendered possible communion with that act which intimately characterised his own existence: dialogue with the Father. This is what is most profound in his method of teaching his disciples to say "Our Father".

This being so, then communion with the life of Jesus and the consequent knowledge of Jesus presuppose communication with the living subject of the tradition to which all this is ordained, communication with the Church. Jesus' message could never otherwise live nor communicate life save by this participation. The New Testament also presupposes the Church as its subject. It grew out of the Church and in the Church; it finds its unity only in the faith of the Church, faith which draws diverse elements into unity. This bond of tradition, knowledge, and communion of life, appears in all the New Testament writings. In order to express this, John, in his Gospel and in his Letters, coined the figurative ecclesial 'we'. Thus for example in the final verses of his first letter, the formula 'we know' (Jn 5,18-20) occurs three times. It is found also in the conversation between Jesus and Nicodemus (Jn 3,11), and each time refers to the Church as the subject of knowledge of the faith.

The same function is to be met in the concept of 'memoria', contained in the fourth Gospel. With this word, the Evangelist points to the interlacing of tradition and knowledge. But it also

126

makes clear, in the first place, that development and defence of the identity of the faith go together. This thinking could also be outlined as follows: The tradition of the Church is that transcendental subject in which the memory of the past is present. Therefore with the passage of time, what is already held in memory can be clearly seen and be better understood in the light of the Holy Spirit who leads to the truth (Jn 6,13; cf. 14,26). This advance is not a coming to birth from something totally new, but a process in which the memory 'enters' within itself.

This bond of religious knowledge, the knowledge of Jesus and of God through the community memory of the Church, does not in any way eliminate the personal responsibility of the reason, nor does it put any obstacle to it. It forms on the contrary the hermeneutic basis for rational comprehension; it brings about a fusion between the one and the other, and thus leads on to comprehension. This memory of the Church lives from the fact that it comes to be enriched and deepened by the experience of the love which is adoration, but also the fact that it always emerges purified when under reasoned criticism. The ecclesial aspect of theology deriving from what has been said is not, then, a cognitive collectivism nor an ideology violating reason, but a hermeneutic interval which the reason needs in order to be able to act. And thus we return to our starting point: Jesus and the Church, the Christological mystery and the mystery of the Church, are inseparable; the Church, the People of God, really is the 'body of Christ', present in history until the end of the world.

2. Pentecost — the beginning of the Church in the sending of the Holy Spirit

A first sketch of a catholic ecclesiology is found in the Acts of the Apostles; this is also admitted today by the Protestant exegetes, who call St Luke *frühkatholisch* (primitive catholic) and criticise him for it. St Luke develops his course of ecclesiology in the first two chapters of Acts, especially in the account of Pentecost day. I should like therefore to give briefly in this conference a general view of the principal elements of this ecclesiology, starting from the account of Pentecost as it is presented in Acts.

Pentecost is for St Luke the birth of the Church through the working of the Holy Spirit. The Spirit descends on the community of disciples who "with one accord devoted themselves to prayer, together with . . . Mary the mother of Jesus" and the eleven Apostles. We can therefore say that the Church begins with the descent of the Holy Spirit and that the Holy Spirit 'enters' into a community which prays, is united, and at whose centre are Mary and the Apostles.

Meditating on this simple fact reported in the Acts of the Apostles, we find the marks of the Church:

1. The Church is apostolic, "built upon the foundation of the apostles and prophets" (Eph 2,20). The Church cannot live without the living, concrete bond with the uninterrupted line of apostolic succession, sure guarantee of fidelity to the faith of the Apostles. St Luke emphasises this mark of the Church in his description of the primitive Church once again in the same chapter: "They devoted themselves to ['persevered in'] the apostles' teaching" (2,42). The value of perseverance, of being and living constantly in the doctrine of the Apostles is, according to the Evangelist's intention, also an admonition for the Church of his time — and all times. Note that it is not a matter of only *listening* to the Apostles' teaching; it is a matter of the deep and vital perseverance by which the Church is inserted, rooted, in the *doctrine* of the Apostles; and thus the admonition becomes more radical for the personal life of believers also.

Is my *life* truly based on this doctrine? Do the currents of my life flow in this central direction? The moving discourse of St Paul to the elders of the church at Ephesus (Acts 20) gives still deeper meaning to this element of 'persevering' in the doctrine of the Apostles. The elders are the ones responsible for this perseverance; they are the support on which 'persevering in the doctrine of the Apostles' hinges and 'to persevere' implies in this sense what is linked with it, obedience to the elders: "Take heed to yourselves and to all the flock, in which the Holy Spirit has made you guardians, to feed the Church of the Lord, which he obtained with his own blood" (20,28). Do we watch sufficiently over ourselves? Do we watch over the flock? Do we seriously consider the ponderous fact that Jesus has obtained that flock with his *blood*? Do we know how to value the price paid by Jesus — his blood — to obtain that flock?

2. Let us return to St Luke's account of Pentecost. The Spirit entered into a community united with the Apostles, and this community was assiduous in prayer. Thus we find the second mark of the Church. The Church is holy, and her holiness does not result from her own powers; her holiness results from her conversion to the Lord. The Church looks to the Lord and thus comes to be transformed in his image. "Let us fix our gaze firmly on the Father and Creator of the whole world", writes St Clement of Rome in his letter to the Corinthians (19,2); and another significant passage in the same letter says: "Let us keep our eyes fixed on the blood of Christ" (7,4). Fix our gaze on the Father — fix our eyes on the blood of Christ: this perseverance is the essential condition of the Church's stability, her fertility, her life.

Again, this matter of the Church's image is repeated and deepened in the description of the Church at the end of the second chapter of Acts: "They devoted themselves — St Luke says here — to the breaking of bread and to the prayers". By celebrating the Eucharist we keep our eyes fixed on the blood of Christ. Thus we shall also see that the celebration of the Eucharist is not a purely liturgical thing but that it has to be the fixed centre of our life. Starting from this centre we become "conformed to the image of his Son" (Rom 8,29). It is thus that the Church becomes holy and, in holiness, one. St Clement gives the formula "Let us fix our gaze on the blood of Christ" also in these other words: "Let us convert ourselves sincerely to his love". To fix our gaze on the blood of Christ is to fix our gaze on love, and become loving.

3. With these considerations let us return to the event of Pentecost: the community at Pentecost was united in prayer, was "in one accord" (1,14). After the descent of the Spirit, St Luke uses a still stronger expression: "the company . . . were of one heart and one soul" (4,32). And with these words St Luke indicates the deeper reason for the union in the

primitive community: oneness of heart. The heart — the Fathers of the Church tell us — is the driving-force of the body *tó egemonikón* according to stoic philosophy. This essential organ, this centre of our life, after conversion no longer acts of its own volition as the private and isolated 'I' of the individual, seeking itself and making itself the centre of the world. The heart, the driving force, is one and unique for all and in all: "It is no longer I who live, but Christ who lives in me" (Gal 2,20), says St Paul, expressing the same thought, the same reality: when the centre of myself is outside myself, the prison of the 'I' is laid open and my life begins to share in the life of another — Christ — when this hapens it produces unity.

There is a close link between this point and those preceding. To transcend our own life demands the way of prayer, not only private prayer but the prayer of the Church — that is the Sacrament and the Eucharist, active union with Christ. And to follow in the way of the Sacraments demands perseverance in the doctrine of the Apostles, and with the successors of the Apostles, with Peter. But another element must enter in, the Marian element — oneness of heart: daily life, feelings, will and intellect, intimately penetrated by the life of Jesus.

4. Pentecost day supplies also the fourth mark of the Church — catholicity. The Holy Spirit shows his presence in the gift of tongues, thus renewing and reversing the occurrence at Babel: the pride of the people who wanted to become like God and build the Tower, the bridge to heaven, with their own powers, without God. It is this pride which creates the divisions in the world, the walls of separation. In their pride men and women recognise only their own intelligence, their own will, their own feelings, and in consequence are no longer able to understand the language of others or to hear the voice of God. The Holy Spirit, divine love, understands tongues and makes them understood; he gives unity in diversity. Thus already on her first day the Church speaks in all languages; she is catholic from the start. The bridge between heaven and earth exists: the Cross is that bridge; the love of the Lord built that bridge. The construction of that bridge surpasses all the possibilities of technology; the Babel attempts had to founder, and must

still. Only the incarnate love of God could build it. Where heaven is open and the angels go up and down (cf. Jn 1,51), men and women begin again and understand one another.

The Church is catholic from the first moment of her existence, embracing all tongues. In St Luke's idea of the Church and consequently in an ecclesiology faithful to Scripture, the sign of tongues expresses something very important: the Church universal precedes the particular Churches, the whole comes before the parts. The Church universal is not a secondary fusion of local Churches; the Church universal, catholic, gives birth to the particular Churches, which can remain Churches only in communion with catholicity. On the other hand: catholicity requires the multiplicity of tongues, the reconciliation and reunion of the wealth of humankind in the love of the Crucified. Catholicity is not therefore only an external thing, but also an internal characteristic of personal faith: it is believing with the Church of all times, all continents, all cultures, all languages. Catholicity demands an open heart, as St Paul says to the Corinthians: "You are not restricted by us, but you are restricted in your own affections. In return — I speak as to children — widen your hearts also" (2 Cor 6,12-13). This 'widen your hearts' is the enduring imperative of catholicity. The Apostles were able to bring about the catholic Church because in their hearts the Church was already catholic. Their faith was catholic, open to every tongue. The Church becomes barren where and when she lacks catholicity of heart, catholicity of personal faith.

For St Luke the day of Pentecost anticipates the whole history of the Church. This history is in its entirety a manifestation of the Holy Spirit. The realisation of the Holy Spirit, driving the Church to the uttermost ends of the earth and throughout all ages, is the central theme of every chapter of Acts, wherein is described the transition of the Gospel from the Hebrews to the pagans, from Jerusalem to Rome. In the structure of this book, Rome stands for the pagan world — all the peoples who are outside the ancient people of God. It concludes with the arrival of the Gospel in Rome, not because the end of St Paul's process is without interest but because this book is not a novel. With the arrival in Rome the journey begun in Jerusalem has reached its goal; the

Church catholic, which continues and substitutes the ancient people of God centred in Jerusalem, has been realised. In this sense, Rome is already in the ecclesiology of St Luke given an important theological significance, and becomes part of the lucan concept of the catholicity of the Church.

Thus it can be said that Rome is the name of catholicity. The binomial 'Roman Catholic' expresses no contradiction, as though the name of a particular Church, a city, were a restricting or even withdrawing of catholicity. Rome means fidelity to the origins, to the Church of all ages, and to a Church which speaks in all tongues. But for Rome to have such a spiritual content means for us, who are called to be this Rome today, the guarantee of genuine catholicity and an obligation which demands much of us.

This consists in a deep committed fidelity to the successor of St Peter, and an inner journey towards an ever more profound catholicity — and also the readiness at any time to accept the state of apostle as described by St Paul: "For I think that God has exhibited us apostles . . . as last of all, like men sentenced to death; because we have become a spectacle to the world — as the refuse of the world, the offscouring of all things" (1 Cor 4,9,13). Anti-Roman sentiment on the one hand results from sin, human weakness and human errors, and so is always a fresh subject for examination of conscience and an incentive to great and sincere humility; on the other hand this sentiment corresponds to the situation of the Apostles and so is a great source of consolation. We know the Lord's saying: "Woe to you, when all men speak well of you, for so their fathers did to the false prophets" (Lk 6,26).

The words used by St Paul when he wrote to the Corinthians come to mind here: "Already you are filled! Already you have become rich!" (1 Cor 4,8). The apostolic ministry is not compatible with this type of satiation, with false praise at the expense of truth, which would be to disown the Lord's Cross.

Finally, to sum up: St Luke's ecclesiology is, as we have seen, a pneumatological ecclesiology and thus fully Christological — a spiritual ecclesiology and at the same time concrete and juridical too — a liturgical and personal ecclesiology, and ascetical. It is relatively easy to understand this synthesis of St Luke's, with our intellect; but it is the work of a life-time, an obligation to live this synthesis more and more and thus really become catholic.

3. The Church is communion

In this third conference on the mystery of the Church I propose a meditation regarding a key-word in ecclesiology, one which expresses in a remarkable manner the inseparability of Christ and his Church, of the Church universal and particular Churches, of the sacramentality of the Church and the experience of the local community; the word *communio*.

a) *The Christian significance of the word and its roots*

A brief analysis of the roots of the Christian usage of the word 'communion' can show us how the stages of development in the human spirit are directed towards Christ and how in the Lord is realised the synthesis of separate or even opposed elements in human thought.

1. A primary origin of the Christian word *communio* appears to be a long way off from the religious and spiritual world, but it is precisely this profane root which has become important; we shall meet it in our last meditation, and therefore I will limit myself here to a brief reference.

In the account of St Peter's call (Lk 5,10) we read that James and John, the sons of Zebedee, were *koinonoi* of Simon, that is his 'partners' in the fishing. In other words: the three constitute a 'cooperative', they are proprietors of a small enterprise, of which Simon is the manager. "You shall be fishers of men": in the conference on the priesthood we shall meditate on the marvellous transformation of this cooperative of Simon's into the 'communion' of the Church. The fishing *koinonia* (communion, cooperative) becomes the *koinonia* of the fish wrapt in mystery, Christ.

2. The second root of the Christian word *communio* is to be found in the Hebrew world. In our meditation of Holy Thursday we have already shown that the *chaburah* of the Hebrews corresponds to the *koinonia* of the Greeks; this word,

too, indicates a cooperative, a society of common *work* and common *values*. But naturally the particular situations of Hebrew society are reflected in the word, adding specific aspects to its meaning. Essentially there are three. The Pharisees as a group already called themselves *chaburah* in the first century BC; the Rabbis came to be called the same by the end of the second century; and finally also the community gathered in for the Passover meal (at least ten people). In this last significance the mystery of the Church appears again. The Church is the *chaburah* in a very profound sense: it is the community of Jesus' Pasch, the family that fulfils his eternal desire to eat the Pasch with us (cf Lk 22,15). His Pasch is more than a meal: it is love unto death. His Pasch is therefore the participation in his own life, shared in his death for all, communicated in this anticipation of death which is realised when he says, "Take this, all of you, and eat it: this is my body which will be given up for you. Take this, all of you, and drink from it: this is the cup of my blood, the blood of the new and everlasting covenant. It will be shed for you and for all so that sins may be forgiven".

Here we find in a very clear fashion what is specific of the New Testament, what is new in the 'New'. In the Old Testament also the ultimate intention of sacrifice and meal is the communion between God and his people. But the word *chaburah* — communion — is never used to express the relation between God and the human race; it means exclusively relations between human beings. Between God and humans there is no communion: the transcendence of the Creator is insuperable. The relationship actually existing between God and human beings is not expressed by the word 'communion' but with the term 'covenant' (testament: *berith*). This terminology signifies both the superiority of God, who alone can take the initiative of forming a relationship, and the distance permanent within the relationship. For that reason some exegetes refuse to translate *berith* as covenant: covenant expresses a certain equality between the partners, which on the contrary does not exist in the relation between God and human beings. In conclusion, the Old Testament *does not know* a communion between God and the human race; the New Testament conversely *is communion*.[1]

3. While the Old Testament opposes the transcendence and the uniqueness of God to pagan polytheism, and has consequently to reject the beautiful concept of communion between God and humankind, in the pagan world this concept was central to religion. Plato speaks in his *Symposion* of the reciprocal communion between the gods and men and explains that this communion is the ultimate intention and the most profound content of the sacrifice, of worship. In the final analysis, he says, worship is concerned with nothing else than love's care and cure.[2] What a foreshadowing of the truth of Christ! Let us add that for Greek mysticism also communion between the divinity, human beings, and all rational beings, is a central concept, but the true desire of this mysticism is union, not communion, with the divinity: in the end it is identity, not relation. If Philo distances himself from the traditional Hebrew terminology and in the framework of Greek mysticism he too speaks of the *koinonia* between God and worshipper, we may well speak of a certain hellenisation of Hebrew thought. But if in the New Testament the Church is communion, not only between persons but, by means of the mystery of death and resurrection of Jesus, it is communion with Christ, man and Son of God — and therefore with the eternal love of the Trinity — this is not the result of a new thought synthesis but rather the fruit of a new reality. The one and only transcendent God of the Old Testament reveals his inmost life; he reveals that he is in himself the eternal dialogue of love. Since he is in himself relation, he is word and love and therefore can speak, listen, respond, love. Since he is relation, he can open himself to a relation of the creature with himself. In the Incarnation of the eternal Word is realised that communion between God and humankind that at first seemed incompatible with the transcendence of the one and only God.

Plato's affirmation that things pertaining to worship are concerned with communion between the gods and the human race and that all this belongs to the safeguarding and healing of love, now takes on a new significance. Let us note that Plato is not speaking of God but of gods, and that Greek mysticism also does not speak of God but of the divinity. In Jesus we have something totally new: that the one and only personal God really communicates with human beings, incarnating himself in human nature. Divine nature and human nature compenetrate — 'inconfuse et indivise' — in the person of Christ. It would be absurd to want to see here a hellenisation of Christianity out of a desire to return to pure Hebrew origins. To do such a thing would be simply to renounce the newness of Christianity. In reality the Incarnation is the new synthesis drawn by God himself, going beyond the limits of the Old Testament, assuming the whole heredity but bringing to it the riches of every culture: the Incarnation is reconciliation, it is communion of those once at enmity (cf Eph 2,11-22), of Jews and pagans, and in the field of thought as well. The charge of hellenisation and the purist return to hebraic origins signify a want of comprehension of the essence of Christianity.

4. In 1 Cor 10,16ff we find the heart of Christianity explained by means of the word 'participation' — communion. In this passage of Scripture the central premise of our argument finally appears: the enduring origin of ecclesiastical communion is founded on Christology; Christ Incarnate is the communion between God and humankind; the essence of Christianity is fundamentally nothing other than participation in the mystery of the Incarnation, or, using a formula from St Paul, the Church, as Church, is the body of Christ. If we accept this truth the indivisibility of Church and Eucharist, communion and community, is entirely clear. In the light of this statement the words of St Paul concerning our problem, or better, our mystery, are explained without difficulty. "The cup of blessing which we bless, is it not a participation in the blood of Christ? Because there is one bread, we who are many are one body, for we all partake of the one bread" (1 Cor 10,16ff). For St Augustine these verses formed the core of his theology, and his homilies for Easter are in fact an exegesis of these words. By eating the same bread we become what we eat. This bread — he says in his *Confessions* — is the food of the strong. The usual foods are less strong than the person taken them and in the last analysis this is to their purpose: they are assimilated into the organism of the one eating them. But this food is superior to the person taking it, it is the stronger, and therefore the purpose is inverted: the person

becomes assimilated to Christ, becomes bread like him: "We being many are one bread, one body". The consequence is obvious: the Eucharist is not a dialogue for two only, a private meeting between Christ and myself: Eucharistic communion is a total transformation of my life. This communion discloses the 'I' of a person and creates a new 'we'. Communion with Christ is necessarily communication also with all 'his'; I thus become part of this new bread which he creates by the transubstantiation of earthly beings.

Now we may see the close connection between the notion of *communio* and the concept of the Church the body of Christ as well as the images of Christ, the true vine, or the fig tree, symbols of the people of God. These biblical concepts demonstrate once again the dependence of the community of Christians on Christ. The community of Christians is not to be explained in purely horizontal fashion: a two-way relationship with the Lord is the condition of its existence; we can also say: the Church is relationship realised by the love of the Lord, which creates also a new relationship with us. With the fine words of Plato we can say that the Eucharist is really 'love's healing'.

b) *Eucharist — Christology — Ecclesiology:*
 the Christological centre of our argument

1. The communion between God and humankind in Christ
   — foundation and model of Christian communion.

As a last stage we have now to look more closely at the Christological content of communion, the foundation and source of the Christian community.

Jesus Christ, as we have seen, opens the way to the impossible, to communion between God and humankind, because he, the Incarnate, is that communion; in him we find realised that 'alchemy' which transforms the human into the divine. Receiving our Lord in the Eucharist means entering into the being of Christ, entering into that alchemy of the human being, into that opening up towards God, which is the condition of the intimate opening of one person to another. The road to communion between persons is via communion with God. To understand the spiritual content of the Eucharist we have first to grasp the spiritual dynamism of the God-man; only in a spiritual Christology will the spirituality of the Eucharistic sacrament open itself up to us. Western theology, with its concern for the ontological and historical, has perhaps somewhat neglected this aspect of theology, which is the true bond between the various parts of theology and between theology and life. The third Council of Constantinople, as we have already stressed in our Christological meditations, gives some indications which seem to me indispensable for the right interpretation of the Council of Chalcedon. The teaching of this Council has been explained by St Maximus the Confessor. We may give the essence in a few words: Chalcedon had expressed the hypostatic union of God and man in Christ with its well-known classic formulas. The second Council of Constantinople asked: What is the existential content of the ontological formula? What is 'a person with two natures'? How can this person really live with two wills, two intellects, so infinitely different? This is no purely theoretical curiosity but a problem for our lives: how can we live, as baptised persons in Christ, following the model of St Paul: "It is no longer I who live, but Christ who lives in me" (Gal 2,20)?

Two solutions were put forward; both unacceptable. Some said that there did not exist in Christ a proper human will. The second Council of Constantinople repudiated this Christ as 'weak and weary'. The other solution was a complete separation of the two wills. But by this we arrive at a kind of monstrous schizophrenia, equally unacceptable. The Council replies: The ontological *union* is on the level of existence understood as *communion*. The Fathers thus sketch an ontology of freedom; the two wills are united in a manner in which the different wills can be united: in a common 'Yes' to common values. These two wills are united in the 'Yes' of the human will of Christ to the divine will of the Logos. Thus the two wills become in reality a single will, and yet remain two. The Council says: Just as the flesh of the Lord can be called flesh of the Logos, so his will can be called the will proper to the Logos of God. In practice the Council is applying here the Trinitarian model: this ultimate unity, the unity of God, is not a mechanical unity but is communion, it is love. The Council found its solution in the Lord's words: "I have come down from heaven, not to do my own will, but the will of him who sent me" (Jn 6,38). St Maximus finds the centre of his Christology — in which he develops the practical content of the Christology of Chalcedon — in the prayer at Gethsemane: "... not what I will, but what thou wilt" (Mk 14,36). Here, in the obedience of the Son, in the suffering of obedience, is realised the communion between the divine and the human being. The wonderful exchange ('admirable commercium'), the alchemy of the two beings — here is realised the liberating and reconciling communion. To receive the Eucharist in its deepest significance means to enter into this exchange of wills. In the suffering of this exchange, and only here, the human essence is really changed, world conditions are changed, community is born, the Church is born. The ultimate act of sharing in the obedience of the Son is the only thing really efficacious also for renewal and change in the external realities of the world.

One other observation is necessary to complete our reflections. Let us recall the premises given so far. The Incarnation of the Son of God brings about communion between God and humankind and thus also opens up the possibility of a new communion between people. Communion between God and humankind realised in the person of Jesus becomes communicable in the Paschal Mystery, that is in the Lord's death and Resurrection. The Eucharist is our participation in the Paschal Mystery and thus it constitutes the Church, the body of Christ. Hence the necessity of the Eucharist for salvation. The necessity of the Eucharist is the same as that of the Church. It is in this sense that the Lord says: "Unless you eat the flesh of the Son of Man and drink his blood, you have no life in you" (Jn 6,53). This demonstrates also the necessity for the visibility of the Church and for a visible concrete unity. The intimate mystery of the communion between God and humankind is accessible in the sacrament of the *Body* of the Risen Lord; the mystery requires our *body* and is realised in one *body*: the Church constructed by means of the sacrament of the Body of Christ must itself be a body, and a single body, and, conformably to the unity in the Lord, must be expressed in unity and coherence with the teaching of the Apostles.

139

2. The problem of the excommunicate.

But what are we to say of so many of the Christians who believe and hope in the Lord, those who desire the gift of his Body, but cannot receive the sacrament? I am thinking of the many different forms of impossibility of communion. On the one hand there is effectively an impossibility of participation in the sacrament in situations of persecution or through lack of priests; on the other hand there exists a juridical impossibility, for example in the case of persons divorced and remarried. In a certain sense also the problem of non-Catholic Communions without apostolic succession is relevant to our enquiry. Naturally we cannot here resolve such difficult and diverse problems. But not to mention the problem would be wanting in sincerity; and besides, even if the problem is insoluble, a certain acknowledgment of it can be useful. J. Hamer in his important book *L'Eglise est une communion* demonstrates that medieval theology, which could not ignore the reality of the excommunicate, took this problem very seriously.

Medieval thinkers could no longer equate, as the Fathers had done, belonging to the visible communion with relationship with the Lord. Gratian had written: "Beloved, any Christian excommunicated by the priests is consigned to the devil. Why? Because outside the Church there is the devil, just as inside the Church there is Christ". The theologians of the thirteenth century had to safeguard the indispensable relatedness of within and without, the sign and the reality, the body and the spirit, but while safeguarding it they had nevertheless to distinguish what was in fact inseparable. Thus William of Auvergne distinguishes external communion from that which is interior, linked though they are as sign and reality. This theologian explains that the Church never intends to deprive anyone of interior communion. If the Church applies the sword of excommunication she does it with the sole intention of healing, with that medicine which is spiritual communion. William adds a very consoling and stimulating thought: he knows that for many the burden of excommunication is no less hard to bear nor less terrible than martyrdom; but yet he says that in such a case the excommunicate draws a greater profit from the virtue of the patience and humility than he or she would draw from external communion. St Bonaventure examines this thought further. The Seraphic Doctor raises a very modern objection against the law of the Church which runs thus: Excommunication is separation from communion; but communion exists through charity. No one can nor should exclude anyone from charity; consequently no one has the right to excommunicate. Bonaventure replies by distinguishing three levels of communion; he can thus safeguard the Church's order and law and say with full responsibility as a catholic theologian: "I say that no one while living on this earth can nor should be excluded from communion in love. Excommunication is not privation of this communion".[3]

Obviously it is not to be deduced from these considerations that sacramental communion is superfluous or less important. On the one hand the excommunicated person is supported by the charity of the living body of Christ, supported by the sufferings of the saints who are united with that person's suffering and spiritual hunger, both the one and the others being embraced by the suffering, the hunger and the thirst of Christ who supports us all; on the other hand the suffering of the person excluded, the longing for communion (and community) is the bond which joins that person to the salvific love of Jesus. In both the cases the sacrament, the visible communion, is present and indispensable. Thus is realised here also the 'healing of love', the ultimate purpose of the Cross of Christ, of the Sacraments, of the Church. And it can thus be understood how an impossibility of sacramental communion can paradoxically become a means of spiritual progress, a means of deepening intimate communion with the Church and with the Lord, in the suffering of a growing love kept at a distance from the beloved; while rebellion — as William of Auvergne explains — necessarily destroys the positive significance of the excommunication. Rebellion does not heal, but destroys love.

St Augustine in his last sickness, very conscious of being at the moment of death, excommunicated himself of his own accord.[4] In his last days he sought solidarity with so many sinners suffering from this situation. He wanted to meet his Lord humble like them in their hunger and thirst, he who had written and spoken such beautiful words on the Church as the community in the communion of the body of Christ. This gesture of the Saint causes me to reflect. Are we not perhaps too inconsiderate in receiving the Blessed Sacrament? Would not a spiritual fast perhaps be of use sometimes — perhaps even necessary — for a deepening and renewal of our rela- tionship with the Body of Christ? Obviously here we are not speaking of the specific spirituality of the priest who in a special manner lives from the daily celebration of the Sacred Mysteries. But let us not forget that, already in apostolic times, the spiritual fast of Good Friday formed part of the Eucharistic spirituality of the Church and that this fast on one of the holiest of days, without Mass and without Communion of the faithful, was a profound expression of participation in the Lord's passion, and in the sadness of the spouse in the absence of her Spouse (cf Mk 2,20). I think that in these days also such a fast, intentional and endured, could on certain occasions be meaningful (e.g., on days of penance or in Masses where the number of participants makes a worthy distribution of the Sacrament difficult), and could thus deepen personal relationship with the Sacrament and moreover be transformed into an embrace, into an act of solidarity with all those who long for the Sacrament but cannot receive it. I think that the problem of the divorced and remarried but also that of inter- communion (e.g., in mixed marriages) would be much less hard if sometimes this spiritual fast were a recognition that all of us depend on the healing of love brought about in the extreme solitude of our Lord's Cross. Naturally I do not in- tend to propose a return to a form of jansenism: a fast presupposes the normal case of eating, in the physical and in the spiritual life. But sometimes we have need of a remedy for our sense of routine and our distractions; simetimes we need to experience hunger — spiritual and corporal — to appreciate once again the Lord's gifts and to understand the suffering of our brothers and sisters who are hungry. Bodily and spiritual fasting is a vehicle of love.

Chapter 2

Meditation on the priesthood

In the last twenty years there has been a good deal of thinking on the priesthood; but there has also been much adverse debate. In such discussions the fact has increasingly been apparent that the many hasty arguments are seeking to eliminate the priesthood as ill-informed sacralisation, and to substitute for it simple temporary offices, functional in character. Slowly their premises are becoming evident which at first seemed to make such arguments almost unopposable. The overcoming of prejudice once again makes possible a deeper understanding of the biblical data in their intrinsic unity of Old and New Testaments, Bible and Church, so that we are no longer constrained to draw water from cisterns, only for it to leak rapidly through cracks of hypothesis and suddenly collect again in little scattered patches, but can now find access to the living fountain of the Church's faith throughout the ages.

It can easily be seen that in the future it will be most essential to solve this precise problem: What is the authentic reading of Scripture? In that period when the Canon was being drawn up, which corresponds moreover to the period of formation of the Church and its catholicity, Irenaeus of Lyons was the first to engage in this question. On the solution of this question depends the possibility or impossibility of continued life for the Church. Irenaeus recognised in his time that the breaking of the Bible to bits as well as the separation of Bible and Church were the element in Christianity and in Enlightenment (so-called Gnosis) that threatened to destroy the Church of the time at its foundations. Earlier, before such fundamental two-fold divisions as these, there had been internal subdivision of the Church into communities which in their turn, by means of a selective use of sources, managed to legitimise themselves.

Splitting up the sources of the faith brings with it divisions in communion and vice versa. Gnosis, which seeks to introduce separation of the Testaments, separation of Scripture from tradition, division of enlightened Christians from the non-enlightened, as an authentic rational principle, is in reality a phenomenon of decadence. Unity of the Church, on the other hand, renders visible the unity of that which constitutes the reason of its existence, and, conversely, in order to live, it needs the strength drawn from the totality, from the multiform unity of the Old and New Testaments, Scriptural tradition and faithful realisations of the Word. Once it has yielded to the logic of decadence however it is no longer basically possible to connect things together again.

Nevertheless it is not opportune to tackle this theological dispute here, though it must be done elsewhere, but to limit myself to making a spiritual meditation, starting from the biblical testimonies which I intend to expound without making use of any scientific critical apparatus but accentuating the aspects which seem to me to belong to the priestly life.

1. Reflections of a priestly image in the accounts of the call in Luke 5,1-11 and John 1,35-42[5]

For my first text I have selected Luke 5,1-11. Here we are told how crowds were pressing around Jesus because they wanted to hear the word of God. He is standing at the edge of the lake, the fishermen are washing their nets, and Jesus goes out in one of the two boats which are there, in Peter's boat. Jesus asks him to draw out a little from the land, sits down in the boat and teaches. Peter's boat becomes the cathedra of Jesus Christ. Then he tells Simon to pull out to deep water and let down the nets for a catch. The fishermen have tried on their own, all night, without success; it would seem useless to start fishing again, now in the morning. But Jesus has already become for Peter so important, so over-riding, that he risks saying: "At your word I will do it!" The word of Jesus has become more real than what appears sure and real empirically. The Galilean morning, its freshness breathing through this description, becomes the image of the new Gospel morning after the night of delusions in which our work, our good will, are continually entangled.

When, then, Peter and his companions returned to the shore with the boats laden and had managed to haul in the results of the catch — but only *together* because of the superabundance of the gift which was breaking their nets — Peter had not only made a journey outwardly and completed a job of work; this trip had become for him an interior journey the extent of which is expressed by Luke in two words. What the Evangelist actually tells us is that before the miraculous draught of fish Peter had called the Lord *'Epistáta'*, which is to say Master, Rabbi, someone who teaches. But on his return he falls on his knees before Jesus and no longer calls him Rabbi but *'Kyrie'*, Lord, using of him the title reserved for God. Peter had made the journey from Rabbi to Lord, from Master to Son of God. After this interior pilgrimage he is in a position to receive his call.

Here a comparison with John 1,35-42 seems necessary, that is, the first account of the calling in the fourth Gospel. There we are told how the two first Disciples — Andrew and another whose name is not recorded — join Jesus, struck by the Baptist's words: "Behold the Lamb of God! " They are struck either by the recognition of being sinners which resounds in these words, or by the hope that the Lamb of God saves sinners. Their sense of unsureness is clearly visible: that they will follow him is as yet uncertain, doubtful. They come up to him guardedly, without saying anything; it seems that they have not the courage to ask. So it is he who turns to them, saying: What do you seek? Their answer still sounds embarrassed, a little hesitant and troubled, but it goes straight to the essential: "Rabbi, where do you live?" or rather, in a more precise translation, "Where are you *staying*?" Where is your dwelling, your abode, where are you, so that we can join you? And here it comes to mind that the word 'stay' is one of the more meaningful expressions in St John's Gospel.

Jesus' reply is commonly translated: "Come and see! " More exactly it means: "Come, and you shall *become* people that see! " They would, that is, be made capable of seeing. This corresponds also to the conclusion of the second account of the call, that of Nathanael, who hears it said at the end: "You shall see greater things than these" (1,50). Becoming capable of seeing is therefore the point of the coming; to come means to enter his presence, to be seen by him and to see together with him. Over his dwelling in fact the heavens open, the secret place where God is (1,51); there we can dwell in the holiness of God. "Come and you will be introduced to vision", which corresponds also to the Church's communion psalm: "Taste and see that the Lord is good" (Ps 34,8). The coming, and only the coming, leads on to sight. Tasting opens the eyes. As once in paradise the taste of the forbidden fruit had unhappily opened the eyes so now also we have the contrary, that to savour the truth opens the eyes so as to see the goodness of God. Only by coming, by dwelling with Jesus, is sight realised. Without taking the risk of coming it is not possible to see. John notes: it was about the tenth hour, the fourth hour of the afternoon (1,39), so already a late hour, a time at which it might be thought it was no longer possible to start anything, an hour at which, however, something decisive occurs not to be deferred. According to an apocalyptic calculation this hour was considered the last hour. Anyone coming to Jesus enters into something definitive, the fulness of time, the definitive hour, the end of time; attains to the parousia, the already present reality of the Resurrection and the Kingdom of God.

In the 'coming', therefore, is realised the 'seeing'. In John this is unfolded in the same way as in Luke, as we have noticed. To Jesus' first words both replied "Rabbi". When they return after being with him, Andrew says to his brother Simon: "We have found the Christ" (1,41). Coming to Jesus, staying with him, he too had covered the road from Rabbi to Christ, in the Master he had learned to see the Christ, and this cannot be learnt except by staying with him. Thus appears evident the close unity between the third and fourth Gospels: both times, trusting in the word of the Lord, which opens the dialogue, they dare to go with him. Both times life is experienced by relying on his word and both times the interior journey follows in such a way that from 'come' is born 'see', which makes of the coming a seeing of the Lord.

Unlike the Apostles' journey, *we* have already started our journey with the *full* testimony of the Church which believes in the Son of God, but the condition of our seeing remains for us too a similar coming, always to be renewed 'at your word'', a like going towards him where he dwells. And only one who sees in person, not only through the witness of others, can call others. This coming, the daring to trust oneself to his word, is still today, and always will be the indispensable condition of apostleship, of the call to priestly service. We shall always need to ask him afresh: Where do you dwell? We shall always need to start out again spiritually on the road to where he is. We too shall always have to cast the nets over again at his word even when it seems senseless. The principle will always remain true that his word must be held more real than any reality that we consider real: statistics, technology, public opinion. Often we shall have the feeling that it is now the tenth hour and that we have to postpone Jesus' hour. But precisely then can it become the time when he is near.

Let us consider again those elements which are common to the *two* accounts of the call. Both the disciples John speaks of let themselves be called at the word 'Lamb'. Evidently they have had some experience and *know* themselves to be *sinners*. And this is not a vague religious expression for them but something which moves them to their depths; it is a reality for them. It is precisely because they know this, that therefore the Lamb becomes their hope, and therefore they begin to follow him. When Peter returns with the abundance of fish, something unexpected happens. He does not, as might be imagined, throw his arms around Jesus' neck for the good success of the undertaking, but throws himself before Jesus' feet. He does not hold on to him so as to have a guarantee of success later on as well, but distances himself from him because he fears the power of God. "Depart from me, for I am a sinful man" (5,8). Where God is experienced, human beings recognise their condition as sinners and only then, while they are truly recognising this and admitting it, do they see themselves in truth. But precisely so do they become true. Only when one knows oneself to be a sinner and has understood the tragedy of sin can one then understand also the call: "Repent, and believe in the Gospel" (Mk 1,15).

Without conversion however we cannot come to Jesus, nor arrive at the Gospel. There is a paradoxical saying of Chesterton's which expresses this circumstance very exactly: "A saint can be recognised by the fact that he knows himself to be a sinner". Weakening in experience of God is shown today by the disappearance of any feeling of sin and vice-versa: when this disappearance takes place it distances a person from God. Without relapsing into a false system of fear, we should precisely return to learning the truth of this word: "The fear of the Lord is the beginning of wisdom" (Sir 1,16; "the root of wisdom" in 1,25; "the fullness of wisdom" in 1,20). Wisdom, true understanding, begins with the right fear of God. We should start learning this again so as also to be able to grasp and understand true love, what it means that we can love him and that he loves us. Also this experience of Peter, Andrew, John, is then, a fundamental condition of apostleship and thus of the priesthood also. 'Conversion' — the first word in Christianity: only someone who has had personal experience of the need of it can proclaim it well, as a consequence of having understood the greatness of the grace.

The sacramental structure of the Church appears to be of the same type as that we have seen in these texts of the fundamental elements in the spiritual itinerary of an apostle. As the experience of sin is to Baptism and Confession, so becoming seeing people, making for the place where Jesus dwells, is to the mystery of the Eucharist. Prior to the Last Supper, the realism which could assume Jesus' abode to be in our midst was certainly unimaginable. 'Here you will become seeing people" — the Eucharist is the mystery in which is fulfilled the promise made to Nathanael: that we, that is, can see the heavens open and the angels of God ascending and descending (Jn 1,51). Jesus dwells and 'stays' in the Sacrifice, in the act of love, during which *he* goes to the Father and by way of his love restores us also *to him*.

The communion psalm (Ps 34), which speaks of tasting and seeing, contains also the other words: "Look to him and you will be radiant" (34,5). To communicate with the Lord is to communicate with "the true light that enlightens every man coming into the world" (cf Jn 1,9).

Let us consider yet another point common to the two accounts with which we are concerned. The abundance of fish tears the nets. Peter and his men can no longer make it out. Very much to the point is what is said then: "They beckoned to their partners in the other boat to come and help them. And they came and filled both the boats, so that they began to sink" (Lk 5,7). The call from Jesus is at the same time a call to come *together* (a *calling together*), a call to *syl-labethai*, as the Greek text says, to hold one another by the hand, support one another, one helping the other, in order to bring the two boats together.

The same thing is made evident also in St John. Andrew, on his return from 'Jesus' hour', cannot keep his discovery hidden. He calls his brother Simon to Jesus and does the same with Philip, who in his turn calls Nathanael (cf Jn 1,41-5). The call leads one along *with* another. It incorporates them in the following and demands sharing. Every call has in it that human element: the aspect of fraternity, the feeling of being spoken to by another. If we think over the road we have travelled, each of us knows full well that there was no beam of bright light from God shed directly on us, but that somehow there had been an invitation from some one faithful, a being carried along by someone. Certainly a vocation can sustain us only if ours is not a second-hand belief — 'because this or that person said I should' — but when, led by others, we personally find the Lord (cf Jn 4,42). Equally necessary are both the inviting, the leading, the carrying, on the one side, and one's *own* 'coming and seeing' on the other. Thus it seems to me that we ought nowadays to have rather more courage in inviting one another and not to hold it of little account, to walk along together following each other's example. The 'with' appertains to the humanity of faith: it is an essential element of it. In it we bring to maturity our own personal encounter with Jesus. Just as in leading to him and carrying along with us, it is equally important to leave others free, allowing them the liberty for their particular call, even when this appears to be different from what we would have thought of.

In Luke these ideas are extended to a whole vision of the Church. The sons of Zebedee, James and John, are called by him *koinonoí* of Simon, partners, if it can be properly so translated. This means that the three are presented as a little fishing company, a co-operative with Peter as manager and chief proprietor. Jesus, at first, calls this group *koinonia* (*communio*), Simon's company. In the words of his call, however, Simon's secular profession is transformed into an image of the future and the new. The fishing company becomes Jesus' *communio*. The Christians will be the *communio* of that fishing boat, united in their call from Jesus, united in the miracle of grace which gives the riches of the sea after a night without hope. United as making up a single gift, they are likewise united for the mission.

In St Jerome we find a fine explanation of the title 'fishers of men', which, in this case, in this inner transformation of their profession, contributes to a vision of the future Church.[6] St Jerome says that to take the fish out of the water means to draw them out of the jaws of death and the night without stars, to give them the air and light of heaven. It means to transfer them to the kingdom of life, which at the same time is light and gives the vision of the truth. Light is life, since its element, by which human beings live in their inmost selves, is truth, which is at the same time love. Naturally people swimming in the waters of this present life are not conscious of that. That is why they furiously oppose anyone trying to pull them out of the water. They think they are as it were a kind of fish that will die soon after being drawn out of deep water. That, of course, would be truly mortal. But this death leads to the true life, in which one truly begins to find the meaning of one's life. To be a disciple means to let oneself be caught by Jesus, by him, the Fish wrapt in mystery, who came down into the waters of this world, into the waters of death, who has become even fish to let himself be caught by us so as to become for us the food of life. He lets himself be caught so that we will let ourselves be seized by him and find the courage to let ourselves be drawn with him out of the waters of our habits and comforts. Jesus has become fisher of men by the fact that he himself has taken on himself the dark night of the sea and come down in person into the depths of his passion. We can only become fishers of men when we give ourselves totally, as he did. But we cannot do this except when we trust ourselves to the barque of Peter, when we enter personally into Peter's *communio*. Vocation is not a private matter, it is not a pursuing of the reality of Jesus for our own sake. The place for it is the whole Church, which can only subsist in communion with Peter and in that way with the Apostles of Jesus Christ.

150

2. Priestly spirituality in Psalm 16

Secondly, since I deem important the unity of the two Testaments, I should like to take now a text of the Old Testament, Psalm 16 (15 according to the Greek numbering). Verse 5 of this psalm was pronounced, by the older ones among us, at the giving of the Tonsure, at reception into the clerical state, almost as if it were the watchword for having assumed the full undertaking. When I go through the Psalm (it is to be found now in Compline of Thursday), it always makes me think again of how I sought then in my understanding of this text to study the procedure of what I was undertaking, so as to carry it out with a deeper understanding. So I treasure this verse for the light it gives me, and it has remained to this day a personal motto signifying the essence of the priestly state and the way to live it. This verse runs thus in the Vulgate translation: "Dominus pars hereditatis meae et calicis mei: Tu es qui restitues hereditatem meam mihi" ('The Lord is the portion of my inheritance and of my cup. It is you who will give back to me my inheritance").

This passage makes more concrete what was expressed in verse 2: 'I have no good [no happiness] apart from thee!'" It does it indeed in worldly language, pragmatically, and I would almost say not in theological language at all, that is, in the language of the land proprietor and of the distribtuion of holdings in Israel as it is described in the Pentateuch or in the Book of Joshua.

In this distribution to the tribes of Israel the tribe of Levi, the priestly tribe, remained excluded. They were given no land. For them was the saying: "Yahweh [the Lord God] is his inheritance" (Deut 10,9; Josh 13,33). "I [Yahweh] am your portion and your inheritance" (Num 18,20). Here there is, at first, question of a simple, concrete law of preservation: the Israelites lived on the land assigned to them; their land is the physical basis for their existence. Through the possession of the physical earth on which they exist, through the possession of the soil, there is so to say life assigned to each one of them. Only the priests do not draw their living from the agricultural work of a countryman on his own plot; the sole foundation of their life, even physically, is Yahweh himself.

151

To put in concrete terms: they lived on their share of the sacrificial offerings and the other cultic gifts; they lived on what was offered to God, in which they were made sharers because they were entrusted with the divine service.

Thus two forms of physical support are expressed at first. In the general context of the thinking of Israel, however, these necessarily bear on something deeper. The land is for an Israelite not only a guarantee of a livelihood; it is the way in which he shares in God's promise made to Abraham, of his inclusion, that is, in the future vital context of the chosen people. Thus it becomes at the same time a pledge of sharing in the very living power of God. By contrast the Levite remains one who has no land and, in this sense, one who is not supported, who is excluded from the earthly guarantees. He is projected directly and exclusively on Yahweh, as it says in Psalm 22,10.

Although it could seem, at least at first sight, that land is being substituted for God as a guarantee of subsistence, almost as offering an independent form of security, this view is however alien to the levitical concept of life. God alone is the direct guarantee of life; even earthly physical life is founded on him. If there were no longer divine worship, there would no longer be sustenance for life. Thus the life of the Levite is at the same time privilege and risk. Nearness to God is the one and only and direct means of life.

Here we have an important consideration to make. The terminology of verses 5 and 6 is evidently the terminology of land appropriation and the different apportioning to the tribe of Levi of what was necessary for their subsistence. It means that this Psalm is the song of a priest who is expressing in it the physical and spiritual focus of his life. The one praying here has what has been established by the Law: deprivation of external property, with subsistence from the divine service and for the divine service, not explained only in these sense of a defined mode of subsistence, but lived in its true basic principle. He has spiritualised the Law, transposed it to Christ, precisely because he fully realised its true content. What for us is important in this Psalm is firstly the fact that it is a priestly prayer; secondly that we find here the inner self-surmounting of the Old Testament moving towards Christ, the Old Testament drawing near to the New, and thus we can admire the unity in the history of salvation. To live not in virtue of possessions but by the sacrifice means for the one praying: to live in the presence of God, in intimate recourse to him, thus giving stability to one's own existence. Hans Joachim Kraus observes very aptly that here the Old Testament allows an understanding of what is required for mystical communion with God, as it develops from the uniqueness of the levitical prerogative.[7]

Yahweh has become, therefore, the 'Holding' of the one praying. The dimension this reality assumes concretely in daily life appears clearly in the following verses. There it says: "The Lord is always at my right hand". To journey with God, to know him to be always at one's side, to speak with him, look to him, and to lay oneself open to his scanning look — this is shown to be at the heart of this prerogative of the Levites. In this way God truly becomes a property, the land of one's own life. Thus we dwell and "stay" with him. Here the Psalm tallies with what we have found in John. It follows therefore that to be a priest means: to walk with him, and so learn to see; it is to stay with him where he dwells.

How this is so, appears still more tangible in the verses that follow. The one praying here blesses Yahweh who has 'counselled' him, and thanks him because at night he has 'instructed' him. The Septuagint and the Vulgate are with this formulation evidently thinking of the physical laws which 'educate' a person. 'Education' is understood as coming to be correctly adjusted to the true dimensions of a human being, which is not to be realised without suffering. The word 'education' would be in this case a comprehensive expression for the direction of a person along the way of salvation; through that process of transformation by which from being clay we become image of God, and so become able to receive God for eternity. The rod of the one who corrects is here replaced by the sufferings of life, by which God leads us, brings us to live close to him. All this is recalled to us also by the great Psalm of the word of God, Psalm 119, which we recite at the Midday Office during the week. Its construction is precisely built around the basic existential affirmation of the Levite's life: "The Lord is my portion" (v. 57; cf. v. 14). And with this assertion the motifs with which Psalm 16 expounds this reality return with manifold variations. "Thy testimonies . . . are my counsellors" (v. 24). "It is good for me that I was afflicted, that I might learn thy statutes" (v. 71). "In faithfulness thou hast afflicted me. Let thy steadfast love be ready to comfort me" (v. 75). So we begin to understand the depth of the invocation which like a refrain runs through the whole Psalm: "Teach me thy statutes" (vv. 12,26,29,33,64). Where life becomes truly anchored like this in the word of God, we find that the Lord 'counsels' us. The biblical word is no longer an indifferent expression, distant and general, but a term which affects my life directly. It leaves history's distance behind and becomes a personal word for me. "The Lord counsels me": my life now becomes a word originating from him. So the saying comes true: "Thou dost show me the path of life" (Ps 16,11). Life ceases to be a dark enigma. We learn what it means to live. Life unfolds its meaning and, in the very midst of the pain of 'being educated', it becomes joy. "Thy statutes have been my songs", it says in Psalm 119 (v. 54), and Psalm 16 expresses it no differently: "Therefore my heart is glad and my soul rejoices" (v. 9); "in thy presence there is fulness of joy, in thy right hand are pleasures for evermore" (v. 11).

When such readings from the Old Testament are put into practice and the word of God comes to be accepted as the ground of life, then comes the contact with him whom we believe to be the living Word of God. It seems to me that it was not by chance that this Psalm became in the ancient Church the great prophecy of the Resurrection, the description of the new David and the one true Priest, Jesus Christ. To know life does not mean applying some technique or other but going on beyond death. The mystery of Jesus Christ, his death and his Resurrection, shine out where the suffering of the word and its indestructible force of life become a living experience.

For this there is no need to make any great transposition in our own spiritual life. Fundamental parts of the priesthood are something like the status of the Levites, exposed, not having land, projected-on-God. The account of vocation in Luke 5,1-11, which we considered first, ends not without reason with the words: "They left everything and followed him" (v. 11). Without such a forsaking on our part there is no priesthood.

154

The call to follow is not possible without this sign of freedom and renunciation of any kind of compromise. I think that from this point of view celibacy acquires its great significance as a forgoing of a future earthly home and the leading of one's own life in chosen and familiar surroundings, and that thus it becomes truly indispensable, in order that being given over to God may remain fundamental and become truly realised. This means — it is clear — that celibacy imposes its demands in whatever setting up of one's life. Its full significance cannot be attained if for everything else we follow the rules of property and of life's game as commonly accepted today. It is above all not possible for celibacy to have stability if we do not make remaining close to God the centre of our life. Psalm 16, like Psalm 119, is a strong pointer to the necessity for continual meditation to make the word of God our own, for only so can we become at home with it and can it become our home. The community aspect of liturgical prayer and worship necessarily connected with this comes out here, where Psalm 16 speaks of the Lord as 'my cup' (v. 5). In accordance with the language usual in the Old Testament this reference is to the festive cup which would have been passed round from hand to hand at the sacrificial meal, or to the fatal cup, the cup of wrath or salvation. The New Testament praying person can find indicated here in a special way that chalice by means of which the Lord in the deepest sense has become our land, our inheritance: the Eucharistic Chalice, in which he shares himself with us as our life. The priestly life in the presence of God thus takes on actuality in our life in virtue of the Eucharistic mystery. In the most profound sense, the Eucharist is the land which has become our portion and of which we can say: "The lines have fallen for me in pleasant places; yea, I have a goodly heritage" (v. 6).

3. The two fundamental consequences arising from these biblical texts

a) *The unity of the two Testaments*

Particularly important in this priestly prayer of the Old and New Testaments is, I consider, the fact of the unity between the two Testaments; thus the unity of biblical spirituality with its fundamental exemplifications appears clearly possible of realisation. Therefore this is highly important, because one of the main reasons for the crisis in the priestly image, both from the point of view of exegesis and of theology, has been the casting off of the Old Testament. The Old Testament came to be seen only in the light of the dialectical opposition between Law and Gospel. It was taken for granted that the New Testament ministry would have nothing in common with the Old Testament ministry. It seems precisely like an unacceptable refutation of the catholic concept of the priesthood the fact that it could be presented as a reversion to the Old Testament. Christology would mean the abolition of any priesthood, the attenuation of the boundaries between the sacred and the profane, the setting aside also of the whole history of the religions with its concept of priesthood as of no importance — as some has actually said. Everywhere in the image of the Church's priest could links be established with the Old Testament or with the religious patrimony of the history of religion: the fact counted as a sign of the decline of the Christian message towards some ecclesiasticism and as proof against the image of the Church's priest. That way there was complete separation from the well-head of all biblical piety and of human experience in general, and relegation to being a profanation, whose spasmodic Christonomonism has in reality destroyed even the image of the Christ of the Bible. This in its turn depended on the fact that the Old Testament itself was constructed as a contraposition of the Law and the Prophets, where however the Law was identified with the cultic and priestly element, and the prophetic dimension with criticism of the cult and with a pure ethic of the human community, finding God not in the Temple but in the neighbour. At the same time the cultic element could then be stylised on the example of the legal element and prophetic piety be characterised instead as faith in the grace of God. In all this, the position of the New Testament came then to be determined: relegated to the anti-cultic, to pure common humanity, and any later attempt to open a door to the priesthood could not in this basic formulation achieve consistent and convincing results.

The theological controversy on this whole thought complex

has yet to take place. Anyone reciting the priestly Psalm 16 together with the Psalms connected with it, especially Psalm 119, sees clearly that a fundamental contraposition of cult and Prophets, priesthood and prophecy, relative to Christology, disappears completely, since this Psalm is at the same time and in the same measure as much a priestly prayer as a prophetic prayer. In this Psalm the purer and more profound aspect of prophetic piety appears evident, and precisely as priestly piety. It is then a Christological text. And precisely because it is this, Christianity in its earliest formation interpreted it as a prayer of Jesus Christ, and felt that Christ in turn applies it to us, so that we in our turn can recite it with him (cf. Acts 2,25-29). In it is shown prophetically the new priesthood of Christ, and from this it appears clear how the New Testament priesthood subsists in virtue of Christ in the unity of the whole history of salvation, and must continue to exist. Beginning with him, it can be understood that he does not abolish the Law, but fulfils it and after having transmitted it anew to the Church, has exalted it in the Church as an expression of grace. The Old Testament belongs to Christ and, in Christ, to us. Only in the unity of the two Testaments can the faith continue to live.

b) *The sacred and the profane*

With this we arrive at the second consideration. Along with the recapture of the Old Testament there is a need to overcome the anathematisation of the sacral and the mystification of the profane. By its nature Christianity is a ferment and a leaven, the sacral is not something closed and completed, but something dynamic. The priest has received the mandate: "Go therefore and make disciples of all nations" (Mt 28,19). But this dynamic of mission, this inner opening out and ampleness of the Gospel, cannot be translated by the formula: 'Go into the world and become world yourselves', 'Go into the world and conform yourselves to its worldliness': the contrary is true. There is God's holy mystery, the Gospels' grain of mustard seed, which does not identify with the world but is destined to be the ferment for the whole world. Therefore we ought again to find the courage to return to the sacral, the courage to discern in Christian reality, not so as to set limits but to transform, to be truly dynamic. Eugene Jonesco, one of the founders of the theatre of the absurd, expressed this in 1975 in an interview, with all the strong feeling of a man of our time seeking and thirsting after truth. I quote a few sentences: "The Church does not want to lose her clients, she wants to acquire new members. This produces a kind of secularisation which is truly deplorable". "The world is going astray, the Church is going astray in the world, priests are stupid and mediocre, happy to be only mediocre people like the rest, to be little proletarians of the left. I heard a parish priest in one church saying: 'Let's all be happy together, let's shake hands all round. . . Jesus jovially wishes you a lovely day; have a good day!' Before long there will be a bar with bread and wine for Communion; and sandwiches and Beaujolais will be handed round. It seems to me incredible stupidity, a total absence of spirit. Fraternity is neither mediocrity nor fraternisation. We need the eternal; because . . . what is religion? what is the Holy? We are left with nothing, with no stability; everything is fluid. And yet what we need is a rock".[8] In this context there are some provocative sentences to be found in Peter Handke's new work, *On Villages*, that also come to my mind. There we read: "No one wants us, and no one has ever wanted us. . . Our homes are empty shells of despair. . . We are not on the wrong path, we are not on any path. . . How abandoned is humankind! "[9] I think that if we listen to these voices of people who are conscious of living in this world it will then be clear to us that we cannot serve this world by means of trite compliance. The world does not need that we agree with it, but that we transformed it with radical evangelisation.

To conclude, I wish to refer to yet another text: Mark 10,28-31. It is the part where Peter says to Jesus: "Lo, we have left everything and followed you". Matthew explains the point of the query by adding: "What then shall we have in exchange?" (Mt 19,27). We have already spoken of forsaking everything. It is an indispensable element in apostolic and priestly spirituality. Let us therefore consider at once Jesus' reply, which is surprising. He in no way rejects Peter's request because he is expecting a reward, but says he is right: "Truly, I say to you, there is no one who has left house or brothers or sisters or father or mother or children or lands, for my sake and for the gospel, who will not receive a hundredfold now in this time, houses and brothers and sisters and mothers and lands, with persecutions, and in the age to come eternal life" (Mk 10,29ff). God is generous, and if we look at our lives with sincerity, then we can see that whatever we have given up he has truly repaid a hundred for one. He does not let himself be overtaken by us in generosity. He does not wait for the next life to give us our reward, but he gives us the hundredfold right now, even if this world does remain a world of persecutions, sorrows and sufferings. St Teresa of Avila has reduced this passage to the simple form: "Already in this life God gives a hundred for one".[10] We have only to have the initial courage to be the first to give that 'one', just like Peter who on the word of the Lord pushes out again into the deep in the morning — he gives one and receives a hundred.

Even today the Lord invites us to push out into the deep, and I am sure we shall have the same surprise as Peter: the fish will be in abundance, because the Lord dwells in Peter's boat — the boat that has become his cathedra and throne of mercy.

NOTES

1. For the historical questions referred to here, cf. the wealth of documentation in the article *Koinonos* by F. H. Hauck in *ThWNT* III; J. Hamer, *L'Eglise est une communion*, Paris 1962; E. Franco, *Comunione e partecipazione*, in M. Simone, *Il concilio venti anni dopo*, I, Rome 1984; J. Ratzinger, *Schauen auf den Durchbohrten*, Einsiedeln 1984.
2. *Symposion*, 188b-c.
3. *IV Sent.*, d 18 p 2a in q 1 ad I; cf Hamer, *op. cit.*
4. Cf. J. van der Meer, *Augustinus der Seelsorger*, Köln 1961.
5. For the interpretation of these two texts I have availed myself especially of H. Schürmann, *Das Lukasevangelium*, I, Freiburg 1969; C. M. Martini, *Il Vangelo secondo Giovanni nell'esperienza degli Esercizi Spirituali*, Rome 1980; J. Hauck, in *ThWNT* III.
6. St Jerome, *In Psalmum 141 ad neophytos*, C Chr LXXVIII 544.
7. H. J. Kraus, *Psalmen*, I, Neukirchen 1960.
8. E. Jonesco, *Antidotes*, Paris 1977.
9. P. Handke, *Uber die Dörfer*, Frankfurt 1981. P. Handke is a young Austrian poet well known in Germany.
10. *Libro de vida*, 22,15.